FLIP THE COIN
AND CHANGE

FLIP THE COIN
AND CHANGE

By Chris Gilbert

Copyright © CHRIS GILBERT 2024

Editor: Caitlin Chrismon

Internal Formatting: SusanSays Design

All rights reserved. No part of this publication may be reproduced, distributed, or transmitted in any form or by any means without the prior written permission of the publisher, except in the case of brief quotations and other noncommercial uses permitted by copyright law.

Dedication

Dedicated to everyone who has poured and will pour anything from a drop to gallons of their resources (time, encouragement, love, money, joy, consideration, patience, etc.) into my bucket.

Table Of Contents

Foreword iii

Intro 1

Self-Awareness or Self-Deception 37

"What Direction Am I In?" Formulas 63

Belief 103

Appendix A 109

Appendix B 113

Appendix C 116

Acknowledgements 119

About the Author 121

Foreword

Chris and I first met at a business networking event. He was selling payroll systems, and I was marketing my landscaping business. In passing, I mentioned being an author among the many hats I wear. Like master connectors do, we decided to learn more about how we could help one another scheduled a one-on-one meeting at a local Starbucks. Chris arrived enthusiastically. Not to discuss either of the companies we had connected about but to discuss his book.

Having written several books myself, I have had many conversations about writing. I have met countless people who said, "I am writing a book." I've been one of those people long before I published. However, when Chris told me he was writing a book, he meant it. He was already 30,000 words in, and the passion for the subject exuded. He could hardly sit still in the chair as he talked about writing and his desire to help others through his story. At that moment, I had no doubt that this book would not only be published but would serve as a compass for many readers. It is one of my greatest honors to have been chosen to write its foreword.

Since that initial coffee, I have come to know Chris well. He's stayed at my home, caring for my four-legged children when I traveled, and shared holiday meals with my family. To say he is someone I trust is an understatement. And trust is critical when taking advice from another human. As you read, you will get to know Chris, his down-to-earth style, and his inherent gift for making the world a better place.

Chris and I don't always see eye to eye. In fact, our views on life are quite different. However, Chris has a natural ability to find common ground, understand another person's perspective and receive and process feedback. One of the last times we visited, before he asked me to write this foreword, we debated the formulas' components in this book. This exercise confirmed for me how clearly Chris envisions the path shared with you. His profound belief that the stories he shares and the process are authentic. This book is the essence of who Chris Hennes, the author, the person is.

The book discusses self-awareness. It speaks of change, of emotion, of success. These aren't concepts learned in a theoretical classroom. These are the life lessons Chris experienced first-hand and the methods he developed for navigating the complications this world brings us.

Having written a growth-related book, I understand that not every concept applies to all people. Each person experiences life differently and takes away something unique and applicable to their situation. As you read Flip the Coin, I encourage you to discover parts that relate to you and share them with others who could benefit from its morals.

If you find yourself in opposition to one of the tactics described, ask yourself what is triggering your objection. When we are uncomfortable, we often realize we relate more to a situation than we care to admit to ourselves. In my work, I often speak of the importance of shifting perspective, or as Chris puts it, flipping the coin. The act of intentionally changing your mindset or putting in the energy to see something from someone else's lens is one of the most powerful gifts we have. We are not locked into any one way of thinking, and the more open you are with yourself, the more you grow. Resistance is an essential clue to knowing when it's a good time to look at something in a new light. When you take the time to embrace change, identifying the real reasons for your beliefs and behaviors are often unlocked.

If you agree with the sentiments shared throughout the book, how can you further embrace the advice and leverage it to grow? How can you make it your own and help to enrich someone else's life? The more we help others, the more we help ourselves.

Like many self-growth books, this guide is designed to be processed over time and tested in real-world circumstances. No book contains all of the answers. Instead, each word provides you things to ponder and reflect on. However, as you absorb it, understand that its writings come from a place of faith and love. They come from someone who walks the talk, experienced the good, bad and ugly, and walked away from it ready to help others.

I am confident that you will walk away from *Flip the Coin* with new tools for overcoming obstacles and a fresh outlook on achieving success.

Jessica Leigh Levin, Author and Connector of People

Intro

"Many receive advice, only the wise profit from it." - Harper Lee

The following chapters aren't me being "holier than thou." This book outlines some of the more flavorful experiences (a.k.a mistakes) of my life, and the nuggets and chunks of wisdom I was able to gain from it. One important distinction, where you read a statement that says "you" know that I am talking to myself also. No condemnation from me, rather instead, a hope to give you information that helps and remind myself of this information when I read this book again and again. If you've been through some of the same experiences I have, or worse, I'm here to tell you there is healing beyond the pain and frustration. It wasn't until Jesus that I experienced true healing myself.

This isn't a hoorah, "fix everything in your life" motivational book. It's à la carte. Take what you like and need, leave the rest. If you draw inspiration or motivation from my experiences, I'm honored and happy for you. If you don't, I won't be offended. I am not going to sell you snake oil. I think motivation comes from hope. If you feel hopeless or without direction, lost in the woods, it's very difficult to become genuinely motivated. I do have more thoughts of potential remedies for that situation later.

However, through my concepts and the wisdom I've gained and borrowed, I believe that hope can be rediscovered. If I've done my job, your motivation bucket will be replenished, and you'll find a new sense of direction. A word of warning though; making someone else your only source of motivation is a very bad idea. If that person goes away or loses your respect, then you no longer have that source. You need to find your own purpose and identity.

That said, this book isn't meant to be a simple "read through and forget it" chuck away. It won't cost you any money to read this book more than once. It only asks for an investment of your time.

I have crafted some tools to remember the large-scale picture of the following concepts for when you need them later. Like a great movie, you see more when you watch another time. This book will be the same for the rest of your life.

What is in this book?

ooo **Challenges**

I'm going to challenge how you see the world and react in certain situations. Above all, I'm going to challenge how you see yourself.

This is a little nugget that I learned from a friend of mine. I told her that if my dad had always been around, not just after I found him at 18, my life would be better. My friend suggested that in order to imagine an alternate universe in which everything was "better", I had to also imagine a universe in which everything was worse.

I had no way of knowing for sure which reality would have happened. All the anger and resentment I had been holding onto faded after three days. Today, I am always looking for false narratives that I've convinced myself. I hope to challenge you to stop seeing situations you see as obstacles against you. Instead, see how they work in your favor.

ooo Wisdom

I've discovered a lot of wisdom from my own twisted road of life. I'll share what others have taught me, because I believe wisdom is a combined effort. There will be quotes from the B.C. era and from strangers I met the week before. One nifty thing about wisdom; it doesn't tend to expire.

ooo Definitions

Redefining words is one of the primary ways I am going to attempt to challenge you and get you to analyze some of your most traditional ways of thinking. We don't realize we do it, but people make up their own definitions and interpretations of words.

Dr. Myles Munroe, a preacher and author, once said that definitions change as we get further away from the origins. These false definitions and interpretations lead us the wrong way. Our interpretations add weight to situations and needlessly increase stress. Sometimes our interactions suffer because our personal definition doesn't match someone else's. By reassessing definitions, you can introduce more clarity into your life, your relationships, and your thoughts.

Our perceptions build our world. Sometimes our perception is wrong. We can solve some of our life problems by getting things defined properly to change our perception! Let's give this a try by looking at the word mindset. Dictionary.com defines Mindset as an attitude, disposition, or mood, an intention, or inclination.

What you don't have is just as important as what you do. NOWHERE in that definition does it say a mindset is CONCRETE and UNCHANGEABLE! While reading this book please treat your mindset like a parachute. It only works when it is open!

ooo Questions

I love questions! There are some people in my life that probably wish I didn't. I believe this is important, though, because we often don't ask questions when we need to. That includes questioning yourself. Please take the time to really ask yourself the questions included in this book. Really think about them.

For a warmup, I have two questions to get us started. Don't worry, these are rhetorical.

Question Number One: why would you listen to me?

Well, I'm glad you asked. My earliest memories of life were within a homeless shelter. Mental and physical abuse was common; my mother took the hit for me whenever she could. Low self-esteem and isolation weren't anything new. They might as well have been family pets. For a time, I played parent to my little brother while my mother battled depression.

I'm sure there's more that my brain has repressed. I know this doesn't sound like an impressive list of qualifications. Statistically speaking, my futures never looked good. I was more likely to be dead, drug addicted, jailed or locked up in a mental facility than anything else. It's easy to blame people for the problems I face. It's easy to live off the charity of others. I didn't choose easy. In spite of my upbringing, I have grown to be a man that has faced fears and won. Even when I did lose, I got up and tried again.

I know what it feels like to have demons you can't even name. I know what it feels like to live in fear of almost everything, to believe you're worthless, to be stepped on and overlooked. I know the agony of looking up and feeling as though you've started so far behind the starting line that you're not sure if you're even in the race. I've lied to myself for years, clinging to the excuses of my past. In short, I've been through the ringer. It's a sensation that people who have suffered through any sort of trauma can identify and connect with.

If I can take some of the lessons learned from these terrible events and use them to help some others, it was all worth it. Sometimes I look back on my life and remember people who have confided their darkest moments to me without even being prompted. Talking seemed like a relief for them, especially when it was a secret that they'd been holding in. I'm glad I was there for them.

Maybe I just had good timing, or maybe I have an innate ability to convince strangers to open up. In that case, I have no choice but to act responsibly and offer my help. It seems as if God gave me the tools necessary to reach out to others. Sometimes, I surprise myself at the wisdom and guidance I've offered (because let's be honest, I'm no scholar).

Yet somehow, I believe I've helped people. Recently I spoke with a victim of abuse. You could see the feeling of worthlessness on them as though someone had draped it on like jewelry. I've been lucky enough to witness their metamorphosis into someone stronger than their suffering. That was all their hard work, but I did offer some ideas that hadn't been considered before. I gave what insight I could about concepts that they hadn't fully thought out. They took those ideas, internalized them, and made the radical change. I'm incredibly proud of them and it feels amazing to have been a catalyst to their change.

Somewhere along the way I developed this innate need to help others. I guess feeling so alone and helpless in my childhood made me want to prevent others from feeling the same. If I can make a difference, then it's all been worth it. If I can push through the self-doubt and truly inspire others that have walked in my shoes, better or worse, then it'll have been worth it (I wear size 14 to 15, by the way, so for those who have walked in my shoes, I'm sorry for the clown feet.)

I was taught an awesome concept in my late teens; a principle called the X Factor. Simply put, the principle asks if you were never born, would the world and the inhabitants be better or worse? I try to always have a positive impact everywhere I can. It's what I was created to do. Just the other day I was in a conversation with a fella that had been a dance student for a decade. He wanted to become a teacher to share his joy. Something was holding him back though: a lack of confidence. Without thinking about it, I started giving him practical mindsets to become confident and excited. The words just tumbled out. Hopefully I manage to help my readers, too.

Question Number Two: Who is this book for? Standby to see if you meet this very exclusive list of qualifications.

1. You have a heartbeat and a functioning brain (these days I know that phrase is a bit loose.)
2. You can read, have someone that can read to you, or can listen to an audible book.
3. You truly want to improve yourself and/or those around you.

Whether you're 10 or 85 (Remember, Colonel Sanders wasn't a success as Colonel Sanders until after 65), my goal is to INSPIRE you to THINK like the person you want to be. I want you to grab the bull by the horns, wrestle and wrangle it until you succeed, then tackle another one. Even further, I hope you'll pass these ideas and concepts along. I have tried to include practical thoughts, concepts, and actions to help you expand beyond the inspirational aspect of this book. It's a tragedy to have inspired to move in a new direction, only to leave them without a path to follow. Look in this book for the inspiration to think larger and do more, but also look for ideas and practical changes to figure out the challenges you face.

To be honest, this isn't a self-help book where I promise that I am going to change your life. I can't change, "fix", affect, or otherwise meddle in your life. Only you can do that. Osmosis might work with some things, but not with knowledge or success. Just purchasing this book, even just reading it, isn't going to make change happen. Trust me, I left my bible on my nightstand expecting osmosis through the dust for quite some time. It never worked. The wisdom and principles found here have to be applied consistently, and this is easier said than done. Success and failure are both required to understand the importance of the advice I will give.

Sorry, I won't lie and say that you will without a doubt achieve everything you set out to do. Life doesn't usually happen that way. While this book has some great wisdom, it won't make you impervious to falling short of goals. Which could be a good thing. There are many goals you will set in life, and sometimes it's better that you didn't accomplish them.

I want to close this introduction with one of my favorite quotes. This is a modernized version of the poem "The Will to Win" by Berton Braley, spoken by Les Brown, and laid out here for you.

"If you want a thing bad enough to go out and fight for it, to work day and night for it, to give up your time, your peace and sleep for it… if all that you dream and scheme is about it…and life seems useless and worthless without it… if you gladly sweat for it and fret for it and plan for it and lose all your terror of the opposition for it…if you simply go after that thing that you want with all your capacity, strength and sagacity, faith hope and confidence and stern pertinacity…if neither cold, poverty, famine, nor gout, sickness nor pain, of body and brain, can keep you away from the thing that you want…if dogged and grim you beseech and beset it, with the help of God, YOU WILL GET IT!"

Chapter 1

I'm Piiiiiiiittt ... Pit fallllllin

"Learn from the mistakes of others, you can't make them all." - Eleanor Roosevelt

I didn't forget how to type with this chapter title. I was going for the chorus of Tom Petty's " Free Fallin' ". This chapter could really be a whole book of its own. Over the years I've fallen into my own share of pitfalls. The truth is, a pitfall can come from almost anywhere, including our parents, friends, enemies, situations, etc. Sometimes it comes from the way we talk to ourselves, dragging our hopes and ambitions down. Whatever the source of your hurdles, it comes down to fault and responsibility.

Fair warning: this book is designed for you to face yourself and do it HONESTLY. As John 8:32 states, "…and you will know the truth, and the truth will set you free."

Before freedom comes truth. For truth to come about, you need absolute honesty. Dr. Caroline Leaf, a cognitive neuroscientist since the '80s, has said that when you admit something out loud it becomes weaker. If it is weaker, it can be beaten. If you keep your troubles locked away inside of yourself, they will stay there, controlling you.

Failing to be honest with yourself means you will continue making the same mistakes and "live life in the past lane."

We'll discuss this more in the Self-Awareness chapter, but don't be tempted to skip ahead. Chapter One is the building block to Self-Awareness. As you get into the meat and potatoes of this book, you might find yourself rationalizing your way out of goals or visions for the future. You might see others doing the same. The foundation you learn from this chapter will help teach you how to throw a rope, metaphorically, so you can pull yourself (or others) out of the pitfall.

The more honest you are, the better your results will be. When the time comes for your testimony and story, listeners will respond to your honesty more than they ever would with lies. Remember that your success can inspire others to tackle their own issues. I'll start us off with a bit of honesty myself; I've struggled with being self-righteous in the past. Maybe others saw it too, maybe they didn't, but I've always thought that I knew the answer to their problem. They would talk to me and I'd think, "well, I wouldn't have done it that way" or "why don't they just—" as though I was automatically right.

Here's the thing, though— there's always more to the story. I was jumping to conclusions when I hadn't even read through all their chapters. Slow down. Remember that no one has all the answers, and sometimes, what your friend needs is for you to just listen.

ooo Pitfall 1: "I Can't."

"As a man thinketh so shall he be." - Proverbs/James Allen

"The Man who says he can, and the man who says he cannot. Are both correct." – Confucius

All our ideas, all our possibilities, start as thoughts in our minds. Sometimes the thoughts are intentional, and others are serendipitous—lucky accidents. Take the lightbulb, for example. It was a fully intentional thought that became an idea that became a possibility. Even so, Edison had 1,000 (other reports have said 3,000) botched attempts at making the first light bulb. His teachers weren't too favorable of him. His mother pulled him from school to be homeschooled, a short 12 weeks after starting school, and he had very serious hearing problems. All in all, not a fantastic start to an innovative legend.

His later years in life still had not-too-promising moments. When he was older, there was a massive fire that destroyed half of his plant in West Orange, New Jersey. Rather than going on a "why me" tirade or "I'm too old for this" rant, he responded quite comically. He told his adult son to get his mother and her friends because they were never going to get a chance to see a fire like that again. When his son commented on the situation, Edison responded "It's alright. We've just got rid of a lot of rubbish," and "Although I am over 67-years-old, I'll start over again tomorrow."

When all was said and done, Edison amassed 1,093 patents over his lifetime. He faced failure a thousand times on just one of those patents alone. Do you think he let "I can't," rule his outcome? Did he let what he didn't know dictate whether he was going to achieve his vision? So then, why do you? The truth of it is, you will fail. That's the point. You learn something new and stretch yourself to a new limit. There was a time you couldn't walk or talk, but you didn't stop learning the first time you fell over. Whoever helped you didn't go, "Well this child can't learn," and stopped teaching you. The very idea is preposterous, isn't it?

So why do we expect perfection as adults? We try, we fail, we quit. It seems like a horribly inefficient system to me!

You didn't know how to walk or talk, and you figured it out. You gave it 110% until 100% was all that was needed. So, whatever goal you're struggling toward currently, make it this simple. Admittedly our goals now have more challenging factors to them, some outside of your control. In certain cases, it's more like learning to walk on a floor that likes to tilt without warning. Still, when you were younger, you never even considered that it wasn't possible to walk or talk. You saw it was possible because others did it, and you believed you could do it, too.

So, take that history of success and apply it. Get your vision together. Clearly put it in your head and on paper, think about it and look at it every day! Stop letting the fear of failure stop you. You will fail along the way. You're learning, and the only way to learn is to just start. Think of it like a marathon; it's finished by taking the first step and not stopping until you get to the end. Give your goal 110% every day until 100% is all it takes. Then set a new goal and keep reaching new limits! If you want something different, you're going to have to do something different.

ooo Pitfall 2: Comparing the worst to the (perceived) bests

This one is so big these days. "Technology is great, until it's not," is one of my new catchphrases. When your phone isn't getting the apps going fast enough or takes too long to answer the phone, you're left wondering about the better phone models out there, the better service providers, so on and so forth.

You may be wondering what technology has to do with anything. Technology isn't just numbers and data anymore, it's how many of us connect via Social Media. Unfortunately, though, very rarely do folks show true selves on their platform of choice, even to the ones closest to them. They sure as hell don't put the good, the bad, AND the ugly part of their lives in their social media feed. Instead, the majority of users muster together a 10 second snapshot of perfection, resulting in a mega fake society where people aren't honest to themselves or others.

This has a major negative effect because now, as a society, we look at everyone else's "perfection" and compare it to our genuinely flawed lives. In short, our perceived reality and shortcomings. There's a couple of problems in viewing Social Media as reality, though. Pictures can be tampered with or set up like a movie stage. Instead of a peek into someone's normal life, viewers are seeing something fake, and are comparing themselves under all kinds of false pretenses.

It is important to look at others and learn from them but avoid using them as a meter for your level of success. Make it a habit to be conscious of the times you are comparing and viewing yourself, your accomplishments, or your goals as lesser than others—then promptly derail that thought train. Overcoming self-doubt and jealousy is a different road for everyone. Some benefit from looking back on how far they've come. Others find it more helpful to reaffirm mentally or verbally, "comparing myself is unhealthy and I won't do it anymore."

It's up to you to find what method works best for breaking the habit of negative thoughts. Remember that you are with yourself 24 hours a day. Your self-talk makes a difference. We become our habits. Spend time on habits that move you forward, not backward!

ooo Pitfall 3: The Road of Success is Smooth Sailing

Maybe it's because of every Hollywood movie in which a plucky young go-getter reaches for the stars and triumphs that some people have this notion of success being easy. They have a tough lesson coming. Success takes long hours of work and change. You must become something more than you already are, which means admitting where you need to improve.

The road to success, however, doesn't need to be seen as something to muck through. The secret to "smooth" success is to enjoy the journey in its entirety. If you treat life's obstacles as fun brain teasers that make you better prepared for the future, you will enjoy life more. Viewing success as a journey rather than an end-goal allows you to continually learn about yourself and improve as a result.

ooo Pitfall 4: "What's in it for Me?"

In general, everyone knows that it's unhealthy to be entirely selfish, but the same is true for being entirely unselfish as well. Whether it's "positive" or "negative", there's sure to be a consequence somewhere. If you live life on the other side of the extreme, only taking and never giving, then you are seriously missing out on one of the keys to life. You get what you give. The energy you give, you will usually get back. The amount of respect you give you will usually receive in turn. I think it's apparent where I am going here.

If you constantly are wondering why people are "out to get you" or "not helpful", well, the problem probably isn't just them. Take some time to mentally, physically, and emotionally present and help others without expecting anything in return. You'll be amazed over time how it comes back to you.

I've found that the best way to pick yourself up is to help someone else. Our minds tend to focus on the negatives unless we give them a new purpose; how better to keep your mind busy than by helping someone else? If you have yet to find a purpose that is bigger than yourself, you owe it to yourself to get out of your own world and serve others. Take this book for example. All this writing is much less about me and a whole lot more about you. I am trying to gift thoughts and perspectives that you can use to grow larger and help others along the way. God and this book are my two bigger purposes I am serving. Even during a 60-hour week, I am able to "find" time and energy to write because the end goal is larger than me.

If generosity and serving aren't natural to you, spend time with those who have these qualities. Emulate them. Think of it like a muscle; you need to work a little bit every day to strengthen it; give up a parking spot, pay for the 2 or 3 items for the person in front of you, hold the elevator door for someone. Sometimes it's as simple as sending a thank you note or telling someone you are proud of them. Giving and serving on a small scale isn't so difficult!

ooo Pitfall 5: Excuses

I wish I could say I came up with this analogy, but I didn't. Still, I hope this illustration is vivid enough that you'll remember it the next time you catch yourself making excuses. Think of a savory stuffed potato; steaming bacon, cheese, ranch or sour cream, and chives just dancing out of it. There's the skin of it, and those delicious carbs and extras on the inside. An excuse is just the skin of a lie, stuffed with reason. Let that concept marinate for a moment.. An excuse is just the skin of a lie, stuffed with reason. Now think about some of the common excuses you make. Look at it from this perspective, and like many of mine I've made, you can see that is truly what the excuse is most of the time.

I'll pick on one excuse that is quite often used: time. We usually have time for what we want to do. We can get up early for a vacation or stay up late for a party (maybe not so much anymore after about age 33 or the first kid is born). For some reason, however, we can't find 15 to 30 minutes for some moderate exercise a few times a week. We all have the same 24 hours in a day. The numbers show that the ones who figure out how to spend a few of those minutes a day taking care of their body usually get blessed with more and higher quality days than those that don't. So truthfully, you are losing more than you are gaining in the long run by making excuses. Whatever skin of the lie you grabbed and stuffed with some hearty reasoning to justify; it has the same result.

It really comes down to the fact that we almost always know what we should do. (Tony Robbins would say to change that word "should" to "must.") The problem is we let that emotional feeling cloud our judgments. Insert whiny voice, "I don't feel like it." Then insert any justification as to why you won't or shouldn't do whatever task you're avoiding. You could just say, "I am not going to do (x) because of peanut butter and jelly." When it's hollow excuses and not an actual reason, anything can be used. Next time you're rejecting something, ponder over if it is as hollow of an excuse as peanut butter and jelly.

If you stop accepting others excuses, they'll eventually stop giving them to you. Warning: They may never talk to you again once they catch on that you refuse to let them lower their standards of themselves. On that same note, do keep in mind that sometimes people do have legitimate reasons that they don't want to share. That's different. Don't swing the pendulum all the way to the other side and be an uppity non-merciful pain in the tail.

No one is impenetrable to making excuses. Recently, I caught myself in the act. My schedule has been incredibly busy for the last few weeks. When it comes to writing, I've only had an hour here or there to put any work in. I would tell myself that an hour isn't long enough. If I'm going to write, I need more time. However, I was able to spend that hour on non-productive activities. I was lying to myself. The skin of the lie was that I didn't have time. I shoved some reason in there— that I couldn't make that time efficiently in what I needed, and it would be a waste— to justify it. However, an hour here and two hours there is better than no hours what-so-ever! Quit telling yourself lies backed up with a hollow justification.

ooo Pitfall 6: Great Expectations

So much damage is inflicted by expectations. We damage ourselves. We damage those close to us. We damage folks we don't know. This damage sometimes grows into resentment and the cycle grows and continues. There are whole books written on this one concept alone, but I'm going to attempt to unpack it in a condensed way for the purpose of this chapter. The damage caused by expectations comes from a lack of proper communication and a lack of reasonable expectations. We can divide this into two sections: self and others.

Self: Lack of proper communication of expectations.

Let's first tackle expectations of yourself. Picture this: it's the end of December and you've been waiting for the New Year to begin some resolution. You tell yourself you'll lose weight or save more money—but you didn't define how much weight to lose. You didn't make a savings plan, write down how much debt you would pay down, or compare your goals to your realistic finances to see what was attainable. You set yourself ambiguous goals, and then felt defeated when you didn't achieve them.

We can see how this pattern could quickly spiral out of control with larger expectations, and how the stress and self-deflating thoughts that spur from it can affect other aspects of your life. If you set a goal, make it clear and measurable, and communicate it to yourself. It's even more effective if you write it down and create a system to keep you on track.

Others: Lack of proper communication of expectations.

A couple is talking on the phone. One says to the other, "Hey hun, stop by the store on the way home and grab some milk."

"Sure babe," They reply, and true to their word, they get a gallon of almond milk.

"I said milk, hun, why do you have almond milk?"

"Because that's what we always drink."

"But my recipe can't use almond milk!"

It's a common sitcom setup for an argument that could have been avoided through better communication. In this fast-paced world, it's easy to know what you mean because you have access to all of your inner thoughts. Remember that the rest of the world does not.

Let's look beyond the scope of something trivial and examine a larger expectation. Two people start dating and don't have a conversation along the way about the number of kids they'd like to have, where they'd like to settle down, or how their parents will get taken care of. Or, in another example, a manager hires an employee with the idea they will remain in their position indefinitely, while the employee plans on continually moving up the ladder. Each scenario leads to conflict, which then leads to damage. Don't leave things under the surface to be discovered the hard way. If you have an expectation, make it known. Public service announcement: it is possible to be clear without being a jerk.

Lack of reasonable expectations.

This applies to yourself and those around you. I believe it was Tony Robbins who said, "Most people overestimate what they can do in a year and underestimate what they can do in a decade." This is very important, so I am going to repeat, and bold it…and underline it. VERY, VERY IMPORTANT.

MOST PEOPLE OVER-ESTIMATE WHAT THEY CAN DO IN A YEAR AND UNDERESTIMATE WHAT THEY CAN DO IN A DECADE.

Set expectations on yourself and others that are reasonable. This doesn't mean you should continually set low goals for yourself, however. Always strive for the highest you can accomplish. It's the whole "shoot for the moon, if you miss at least you're in the stars," idea. Set your expectations at a reasonable level. Properly communicate them to yourself and others.

ooo Pitfall 7: Faults and Responsibilities

Before I really dive into this section, I am going to wait while you search for a Will Smith video. (After originally writing this section, a lot of controversy surrounding his life has happened. Regardless of where you stand on his personal life, this is a really pivotal principle he explains really well) Search for *Will Smith: Faults vs Responsibility*.

I'll wait.

Yeah. Deep. I know—yet it's so simple. In my life I've had to face down the metaphorical barrel of this loaded gun a few times. Frankly, I still fight the effects of faults that aren't mine, such as my parents getting pregnant with me (thankfully) but when they weren't ready. I grew up with my dad not around. Ultimately, it was both of my parent's faults that he wasn't there, but I paid the consequences. In the same train of thought, it wasn't my fault that my brother's dad snowballed our home into a physically abusive situation, but I had to deal with it.

My mother was a great parent, but at times she put the well-being of others above her own, which unintentionally meant others were put over my brother and I as well. Her self-esteem issues, while not exactly her fault, also became mine. It was a vicious cycle that kept her from getting the man she deserved and put terrible role models in our lives.

On the bright side, my brother and I realized you could view people as an example of what not to do. I don't know if it is a term or not, but I dubbed them anti-role models. Instead of making these circumstances excuses (tying these "pitfalls" together beautifully here), I made them reasons to keep putting one foot in front of the other, to continuously grow and push myself further and further. Next time you want to blame someone else for your faults, think about your excuses before you blurt the unnecessary BS from your face. I'm not saying I expect you to never place the blame on someone else. I don't. Just be aware that, as Will says, it doesn't matter whose fault it is. It is for damn sure your responsibility to face it.

ooo Pitfall 8: Making the Task too Large

Excuse me while I borrow another anecdote from Will Smith. In one of his talks, he explains that his father had him and his brother build a brick wall. The synopsis is that they felt it was too large of a task that they couldn't do. It was overwhelming. In the end, his father told him to not lie to himself in the future. He could do anything he put his mind too, if he only focused on it in small pieces (sounds a bit like reasonable expectations, right?) Don't think about the whole wall but instead, brick by brick, do your best with each small task toward your goal.

Take this book for example. It started with simple thoughts and concepts that I think about often. I was having a discussion with a business advisor about collaboration on clients. I asked if some of the concepts I was discussing with him were normal for people to think about. He said "yes, but you do have some unique perspectives." On the way home that day I had a spark of an idea to write my thoughts and their connections down. For several weeks I took notes as I thought throughout the day and built an outline for my book. Then as the outline got more and more details, clear chapters started to emerge. I started writing. At the time of writing this, I don't know what it's going to take to get my work printed and shared with others. I do know, however, that it is going to be several small, smart steps put together.

ooo Pitfall 9: The Carrot and the Stick

Think back to Saturday morning cartoons, the good ones. There was usually an episode or two where an animal is tricked by tying a stick to its back while a carrot dangles off the end. No matter how much the animal walks forward or chases after the carrot, it always remains just out of reach. This is one of the most common pitfalls that keep folks from reaching and achieving new heights.

Recently, I had a conversation with someone about this topic. They had two goals: Goal A and Goal B. I believe both goals were attainable and reasonable, but my friend had made one mistake. They could not, they said, begin Goal B until they had accomplished Goal A. Now, there are going to be plenty of situations where this systematic approach and mindset is appropriate. Prioritizing for maximum efficiency is generally a good practice.

However, I bet there are at least a couple of goals that you haven't achieved or started with this same mindset halting your progress. This cycle usually starts with something like, "once I—" and ends in a "— then I'll be able to." *Once I* pay this down, *then I can* start that business. *Once I* get into a relationship, *then* I'll be happy. *Once I* finish school, *then I'll* live life and start pursing my career (in this age, it's better to prep for your career as soon as possible through internships, research, interviews, and more!)

It's too easy to get trapped in those situations. While you're in the thick of the woods, it's hard to see the whole picture. Which is why we all need a trusted advisor, counsel, or mentor to call you on your BS. An outside view can often see things that we ourselves cannot.

Remember, the phrase, "Once I... then I'll be happy," is one of the most dangerous thoughts a person can have. If you don't find joy in the process, or if you can't find a way to be happy in the now, you likely won't be happy later. Happiness and joy aren't a set of conditions. It's a mindset.

ooo Pitfall 10: Picking it

No, I'm not talking about a booger.

Picking a start date is one of the best ways to begin a new commitment. A bit of advice, though, don't start on the typical January 1st or on Monday morning. That's just a chore, an undesirable thing to do because it's on the checklist. Do you want to be committed? Start on a Wednesday. Why? Because Wednesday was the day you got sick and tired of being overweight, so it's that same Wednesday when you should begin a change. Research what you need for your goals, whether that's diet and exercise or a new career path. Progress can start the moment you decide on your goal.

I'm all for logical reasoning. I prefer it over emotion, honestly. Yet there are times to harness emotion over logic, to use your frustration to your advantage and allow it to propel you forward. Fair warning, the "planning" part of success I was talking about earlier comes in to play here. Your strong emotions will eventually wear away and when they do, you will need to have a plan, discipline, and accountability in place to keep moving toward your goal.

Everyone has something that they've been struggling to start. A better habit, a better mindset, a healthier lifestyle. Something. Quit waiting for me or anyone else to list give you justification to begin. Put this book down and start towards your goal (then come back later and keep reading!)

ooo Pitfall 11: Your Past is a Resource, NOT a Disability

I will give you the same challenge that someone once gave me: write a chapter about yourself and what makes you qualified for your goal. In this, you need to discover what you are using as a crutch. For example, as stated before, I grew up without any good role models. Instead, I had anti-role models. There was no one to look up to for business, mindset, healthy relationships, or anything along those things. I don't consider this my downfall, though. While I didn't have anyone to show me the "right way" of doing things, I did have examples of what not to do, which is almost as important.

This may sound more like a silver-lining than a resource. Admittedly, I still face issues that are rooted in that time of my life. What I have done is taken something that used to paralyze me and turned it into a bruise. Do you know what's great about a bruise? It heals! When I use my hurtful past to help others and guide them through their struggles, it's healing for me. Using my hurt to help them vindicates my past.

What has happened in your life that's holding you back and slowing you down? Is there a different way to look at it and make your experience relatable? Can the hurt you have turn into a passion that will serve others? I'm asking you to step out of the trees of our life and look at the whole forest. Figure out what your crutches are that you have created for yourself and make it your resource! Your past is an asset to your future. If you're a Christian, you may recall Romans 8:28, "...and we know that all things work together for good to those who love God, to those who are the called according to His purpose."

I know since dedicating my life to Him, I've begun to see many of my "bad" experiences as working for my own good.

ooo Pitfall 12: Drunk You Cares for Hungover You, Why Not Have Past Self Care for Future Self

If you are one of those folks that didn't have wild nights out growing up, kudos to you. Personally, I can recall a more youthful, ignorant me (which is thankfully not the case anymore) chugging water and taking pain meds after a long night of partying. There is something nice about knowing that past-you did something to take care of future-you, even while inebriated. Too often we don't take care of our future self! We hit the snooze button 6 times until we're late for our meetings. We don't exercise or eat right. We go about our days trying to hide from pain and discomfort, and when it finds us, we can't handle it because we aren't fighting it on our terms.

Create habits that pay it forward to you! Little steps can make all the difference. Prep your lunch the night before so that you have more time to relax in the morning. Look at your calendar before bed and plan what you want to do the next day so that you can sleep easy. Maintain friendly energy and don't procrastinate— start using the tools in this book today, not "someday."

ooo Pitfall 13: Stop Focusing on the Big "But"

"I would but," and, "If I only had," are common phrases you've probably said once or twice or hundreds of times. Ask yourself, is that "but" a good reason or is it just an excuse? Are the words that follow the "but," the truth? Chances are they are, in fact, a surface level excuse. If you dive into the root cause of why you're avoiding something, you can make a change to your thoughts and words, which will change the outcome.

If you never stop uttering "I would but," you'll never stop making excuses. If you don't stop making excuses, you'll never get what you desire. You may never find out what you truly desire in the first place.

ooo Pitfall 14: It's Hard to Get Where You Want to Go When Busy Complaining

If you are a complainer, then you are constantly finding what is wrong with your life. If all you can do is find what is wrong, you can't see what is right. If you can't see what is right, YOU WILL ALWAYS BE MISERABLE. Misery loves company and is always trying to bring someone else down. **It's hard to live a great life if you can't be grateful**.

Remember that you will always find what you are looking for. The next time you go to utter a complaint, make sure it is merited and will make a difference to have said it. Don't sit there and stew on it. That is a toxic activity that can needlessly ruin your day and everything in it. If an event happens that gives you displeasure or an inconvenience, you realistically have 2 options. Let it harm you, or don't. Harm might seem like a strong word, but I really mean it. Stewing on negative thoughts is destructive to your mind, like drinking a glass full of cyanide is for your body.

Sometimes complaining is disguised as blaming. I'm honestly guilty of this one. Sometimes I catch myself complaining that if this or that wasn't in my way, I'd be doing better. It really comes down to me wasting time and effort blaming everything else when I could be spending more time and effort conquering my problems regardless.

ooo **Pitfall 15: "Well, if you would've just…"**

This is a cousin to fault and responsibility, and I think it does need its own pitfall classification. Since we already covered that life isn't fair, logically we should know most of our problems are ultimately our fault. Blaming traffic for being late really comes down to the fact that you didn't leave early enough.

The more important underlying complication of blame is the precedent that is set. Being creatures of habit, we tend to repeat what we think or do. If we find it okay to blame others for simple things, such as not being on time, then we find it okay to blame others for more complex issues, like having a heart attack or debts. We humans can find a way to blame someone else for almost anything.

Do I think that there are situations where mistakes are legitimately someone else's fault? Of course! I'm simply asking you to catch yourself when you're blaming others and to look at the situation in its entirety. If you had a role to play in the mistake, see what you can do it avoid replicating it in the future.

ooo Pitfall 16: "I like to move it, move it!"

In 2005, DreamWorks animation released a film called *Madagascar* complete with adorable animal characters and dance scene that was ingrained in Americans everywhere. Hopefully, you've seen this film and smiled at the reference.

In later chapters I will go more in depth about action and energy, but for now I want to highlight this as a pitfall. Quite often we attach the feeling of joy, happiness or success to a third-party source, and then wonder why we can't find these emotions. The secret is you won't have joy and happiness until you learn to be happy and joyous without these outside sources.

Have you ever thought, "I should start eating better and exercising more?" You weren't just magically motivated and ready for it, right? You possibly put it off for a few weeks, too. Eventually, though, you did it. You ate right, you exercised, you did everything you said you wanted to do. If you are one of those people, like I was, then you know how great it feels after exercising for the first time. How about day 2 or 3 of exercising? How about day 84?

I don't know about you, but I don't wake up excited to workout. I schedule it and don't question whether it will happen or not. They're ingrained in my day because I need to for the benefits exercise brings. One of the benefits is that after each workout, I feel better than I did before. The movement comes before the feeling.

Motion - the action or process of moving or changing of place or position; movement.

Emotion - any strong agitation of the feelings actuated by experiencing love, hate, fear, etc., and usually accompanied by certain physiological changes, as increased heartbeat or respiration, and often overt manifestation, as crying or shaking.

Do you see the common denominator in this exercise example and these two definitions? MOVEMENT! Try to smile and be angry at the same time. Try being excited and depressed at the same time. It's difficult. For emotions to come out there is a physical manifestation. If you don't like how you feel, move a different way. Try a smile instead of a scowl. Stand tall even if you're only 4 foot 11. Square your shoulders instead of being hunched over in a depressed state. Walk with energy, confidence, and purpose versus uncertainty. Instead of giving that other driver the finger, focus on your own lane or give them a smile and a wave. Control your actions and you will control your emotions.

How much energy and motion do you put into being depressed, angry, or bitter? It's about the same amount of energy it takes to be happy and joyful. Don't believe me? How much effort is put in to running a couple of times a week? How about the amount of effort involved in surviving a heart attack? Paying all the hospital bills? Losing your ability to do the things you could do before? Recovering from getting winded on a small set of stairs?

Why spend the time only putting in half the effort? That's doing enough to be an inconvenience but not enough to succeed or learn what you need. Even if you go all in and don't succeed as you envision. The difference is the lessons you learn will pay you back in the future, but the avoidance is going to hinder you. I talk to people, including myself, all the time about how we're focused on what we don't have or what we don't know. Stop focusing on what you don't know or can't do. Focus on what you do know and can do. There's a lot I don't know and that I can't do, yet. What I can do is put a smile on my face and walk tall, so that I move with confidence and joy!

ooo Pitfall 17: What is that? A book? Where are the pictures?

You would think pointing out the benefits of reading wouldn't be necessary; after all, you are reading right now. I wanted to reinforce that reading consistently is important. Also, I don't mean that it has to always be some sort of "self-improvement" book. Reading about topics or areas you are gifted in, have great interest in, passions and curiosities is great! Fiction books can be great too.

The great thing about reading is you get the experience that took someone days, months, years, or even decades to learn and put together. You get it without the pain that a person went through. I am currently almost 33 years old. I've drawn on self-talk, conversations with others, experiences, videos and speeches, etc. Some of the knowledge nuggets found here I have put together or discovered as I was writing. Most of what I have included are lessons learned as far back as four and five years old. That's almost 30 years of experience in this book, offering a different lens and perspective than you are accustomed to looking through. By seeing how my mind works, your own mind can expand.

Besides the time I spend reading my Bible, I want to consistently read at least 15 minutes a day. I've seen and read studies that the top earners and successful people in the world are reading two and three books a week! What you put in your mind is what you get out.

ooo Pitfall 18: Establish Your Property Lines

It would be nice to meander through life thinking, doing, and saying whatever you want, or at least, it sounds like it would be. If you have children, you've seen what happens when you try to live like that. You end up hurting yourself. As a parent, you've got to establish parameters and guidelines. The goal isn't to be mean and kill the joy of your child, but to keep them safe and set them up for future success. I heard this metaphor on how to explain that parameters help and protect us, and I think it helps illustrate the point.

I have a dog. A beautiful friendly lab— too friendly. She is extremely well-behaved, and I can usually snap or just say her name and she is ready for a command. However, as of late, her friendliness is a problem. I used to be able to say her name and stop her from running up to someone, but now she gets tunnel vision and suddenly becomes deaf when she sees another dog.

If you live somewhere near a road or woods, you probably can't let your dog run wild and free. They may chase an animal in the woods and get lost, not know their boundaries and simply disappear, or run in the road and get hit. If you put a fence up in your yard however, now your dog can run freely inside of the set parameters, without worry.

The "fences" in life aren't there to restrain us, they're there to give us freedom. If you know you are draining too much time on social media, games, talking on the phone, reading mindless tabloids, or whatever is keeping you from productivity...set up some parameters.

Put a time frame or qualifier on the "fruitless" activities. Here's an example: I have friends all over the globe partly because I'm from the gaming generation. I had to set up parameters for myself. I don't play games alone, only with my long-time friends, so it is a social connection. I only play for an hour on a particular evening and only after I've accomplished my tasks of the day.

Now that I have my parameter, I get to have that time to enjoy guilt free gaming because I was productive earlier. Some of you reading this book may think it is time wasted. I would agree, but if you don't take some time to sharpen the axe, so to speak, it stops cutting as well. Work hard and often but sharpen the axe– with some parameters. This is just one small example of not wasting your time. This applies to other resources and vices.

I will put another warning here; our society has memory problems. I once had a conversation with someone about eating healthier. We were going to get dinner and they said, "we should get pasta, we didn't eat anything bad this week." We had pizza two nights earlier. If you truly want to have some high achievement or forward movement on a project, you need to shoot for more time being productive and less time being fruitless. Don't lie to yourself by thinking you hadn't spent that much time on frivolous activities when you spent 4 of your last 6 days not doing what you need to.

ooo Pitfall 19: The Straw That Broke the Camel's Back

Have you ever had one of those days where you just exclaim, "if one more thing goes wrong," or some variant? Usually you get what you ask for, too. I've found when I feel my most suffocated and frustrated is when I am tossing more and more on my back. I do it in this imaginary backpack way too. I have this backpack that can hold an infinite amount of weight, the problem is, it is strapped to me. I can't hold that much weight. You have this backpack too. None of us are impermeable against overloading it from time to time. If you're anything like me, you just keep tossing things in there, pull them back out for a moment, only to then toss them back in. We've got to unpack this can of worms.

Some of this backpack is from us thinking we are computers with unlimited RAM. We keep adding to the list of what we need to do, and it is a mental weight that is continually adding up. One of my favorite phrases is, "if it doesn't get written down, it doesn't get done." Practical step number one to unload this backpack: keep a notebook with you to write these "need to do's" down. Then you have much less floating in your head, taking up space and adding stress. You can easily look at your tasks and see what needs to be done. Then you also get the positive mental feedback of marking the items off.

"But Chris, lists are stupid. I am not a lists person." I get it. I wasn't a list person either. Now I am. If you want to unload some mental taxation, become a list person.

A while ago I had one of those days where I was loading up the backpack. I felt like the Atlas sculpture, the man with the world on his shoulders. I took inventory. Got out a pen and paper and wrote out the items that were a burden. As the day wore on, if more tasks came up, I added them to the list. As I did this, I also wrote out what I was doing or could be doing. Some issues I listed weren't out of my control or weren't as big of a deal as I had built them up to be. By the end of the day, my backpack was lighter, and my back was thankful.

Take some inventory throughout the day on what is going on in your life. List what can be done and what are you doing. You can even put a severity rating system by them. We live in an overwhelming world and society is always vying for our attention. This could be the key to turning a tortuous day into a successful, productive, and less stressful day!

ooo Pitfall 20: Touchdown!

I'd like to see a case study on this one. I would like to know what percentage of the population forgets their victories and lives wallowing in failures. It's a double-sided sword.

Side 1:

We've all met the person still stuck in high school. They were the quarterback or prom queen, and they pin their lives on that success. Their whole identity was who they were at one point in life. Don't be that person! Move on! Get new goals and dreams. I know that is scary, because what if you fall short? There was this one "big" thing that was accomplished and captured in the annals of history. Why move on and risk falling short? Because you can't live in the past. You must keep moving toward something. Without purpose, the soul dies.

Side 2:

If you live in your failures, you learn to focus on only those. What you focus on you almost always end up in. Learn from shortcomings, but don't live in them. When you progress or succeed, celebrate it! I can easily spend 24 hours picking out where I've fallen short in the last three years. I would probably have a rough time picking out my wins. However, in the last six months to a year, I am finding that I celebrate my progress. I've come so far in so many ways! Seeing what I have accomplished in this relatively short time, compounded over time, I can really make a difference in the lives of so many! Take a lesson from me, progress is progress. Limit the amount of backsliding and keep moving forward. Give yourself some congratulations along the way!!

ooo Pitfall 21: New Perspective on an Old History

Long story short, I didn't grow up with my dad around. It never really concerned me as to whose fault it was. At age 18, I decided to look him up. Funny enough, it was a phone book website that led me to find him. I knew his name and that he was likely in Ohio, considering I was born there. I found him on the first try…I was quite lucky. My sister told me her dad wasn't home, and was shocked to hear my reply, "well, I think he's my dad too, and you should have him give me a call." I met my dad and eventually the large family that I without a doubt belong to.

On the surface, that story may seem like an unnecessary tangent, but I am going somewhere with this. After meeting my amazing family and seeing where so many of my traits come from, I went down a thought-path that was terrible. I wasn't as confident as I wanted to be. My childhood had quite a few struggles and pains I shouldn't have had to deal with. My self-worth wasn't anywhere near where I wanted it to be. My introvert nature from my mother was stronger than my extrovert nature from my dad's side, which I was not happy about.

I was severely upset by it all. There was one thought that made it all worse; if I had been with my dad and that family all along, I would be a better person. These struggles I face wouldn't even exist. That anger, frustration, "this isn't fair," feelings were quite the burden to bear. One day I was speaking with a counselor, unrelated to my family but because I had a friend pass away suddenly at our workplace. While the counselor and I were talking, the subject of my father came out. She was quite confused at my belief that if my dad had been around, all of it would have been better, I would have been better.

She challenged me. She said my belief was what I had concluded, but it wasn't rooted in fact. If I was going to play this "what if," game and declare that it was going to be all good, I was also going to have to consider a fact I had not thought of. Perhaps if I had reached out sooner, I wouldn't have been as accepted. Perhaps if I was, everything that I thought was going to be better, could in fact be worse.

I denied it vehemently at first. After it sunk in, I was speechless and I felt a weight lift off of my shoulders and consciousness. When something you have thought was solid fact gets challenged, and turns out to be false, it's like your mind has been suplexed in a World Wrestling Entertainment ring. I left that day with a lot on my mind. When I finally wrapped my head around the fact that she was right, so much weight was lifted. Always be willing to take a new look at an old perspective.

Chris Gilbert

Chapter 2

Self-Awareness or Self-Deception

"Owning our story can be hard but not nearly as difficult as spending our lives running from it." - Brene Brown

Before we begin, I would like to share the definition of a few important keywords to be kept in mind for this chapter.

Self-Awareness - conscious knowledge of one's own character, feelings, motives, and desires.

Character - one of the attributes or features that make up and distinguish an individual; moral excellence and firmness; one of the persons of a drama or novel

Feelings - an emotional state or reaction; susceptibility to impression; often unreasoned opinion or belief

Motives - something (such as a need or desire) that causes a person to act

Desires - too long or hope for; conscious impulse toward something that promises enjoyment or satisfaction in its attainment

Have you ever been in a situation where you talked to someone with poor B.O. and wondered how they didn't smell themselves? Currently, I live in New Jersey, where you're not allowed to pump your own gas because life needs to be more complicated than it already is. The last time I got gas, the fella who filled my car up must've not showered or something because *whew*. I'll be honest, my big ol' nose is mostly just for decoration and my sense of smell is rather weak, so I felt sorry for the people with normal sniffers going to that gas station.

When we encounter this scenario, we usually think to ourselves, *how do they not know?* This is the rest of the world when we lack self-awareness (SA). For my examples to not come off sexist, I am using an androgynous name...Derpy. Derpy can't tell that their tone is out of whack. Derpy doesn't realize that most often, people really aren't talking about them. Derpy doesn't realize we all aren't perfect, and they should quit trying to be.

That image of perfection is like a clean room with a ton of items ready to cascade out of the closet. It's stressful being Derpy, and because they insist on maintaining a false outward image, it's difficult being their friend. Derpy is a know-it-all who doesn't think about things and pops off with emotional reactions. Derpy is stuck acting like they are the center of the universe. Ol' Derps is not looking at things from anyone else's point of view, aka, selfish. (I've been Derpy more often than I'd like to admit)

What Derpy doesn't realize is that although our eyes see the outside world, the way we see that world and ourselves comes from inside of us. We see that world and ourselves as an image in our minds that we developed, which is limited. Limited perceptions have gotten me into some difficult situations that could have been avoided.

Have you ever been sitting in the car at a red light or perhaps in a parking spot, mildly daydreaming? The car beside you moves and your brain has this little short circuit moment; you think you're moving but it's really them. That's where our vision and reality clash. Reality isn't always what it appears to be. If Derpy doesn't take the time to see the whole picture before reacting, problems happen.

I read a story once about this little girl with two apples. The little girl asked her mother if she would like one. The mother says, "Sure, thanks."

The little girl promptly takes a bite out of both apples. If you stop there, the reaction could vary anywhere from laughter, confusion or chastising the child. The rest of the story goes on to say that the little girl gave her mother one of the apples and told her, "I just wanted to make sure to give you the sweeter one."

Insert a long "AWWWW" from the audience and parents. Reacting to a piece of the story vs. listening to the whole story is a cousin to the Expectations section in the Pitfalls chapter. What I am getting at is you need to incessantly work on your SA. In the above scenario, you are internalizing the story as you see it unfold, but only from your perspective.

Now we'll cut a little deeper into this concept. If you are a person that is used to sharing and naturally shares, you might not have even flinched when the little girl bit the apple. However, if you are a selfish person, you would have probably had a negative reaction. Why? Well, we usually expect people to react the way we would. If you are an honest person, you expect other people to be. If you are a liar, you expect everyone else to be as well.

It is very important that you dig deep inside yourself and pull out the truth. This is useful for a multitude of reasons, but here is what I personally believe to be number one; if you know where you are, you're more likely to be able to get where you want to go. What's the first thing a navigation app asks you? "Where are you going?"

That is covered in the formula's chapter with goals. The next thing they ask is, "where are you?" Both pieces of information are needed. If you don't put your actual location and put a wrong starting point instead, — *uh-oh*. The navigation app is going to be confused and so will you. You need your honest starting point.

Some would possibly disagree that the opposite of self-awareness is self-deception. For the purpose of this book and my concepts, that's what I am going to declare as the opposite. I was listening to a sermon after most of this chapter had already been written when I heard the word *self-deception* and had an epiphany. This, to me, is very powerful! If you are not actively trying to be aware of why you think or do or say the things you do, you are by default choosing to live in self-deception. If you are in a season where the gym is important and you say you are not going to the gym because it is raining outside, that is deception in the form of justification. There is a truer, deeper reason. It could be you don't truly believe exercising will help, or that you need to exercise. At worst, you are lazy and refuse to change. (There is also a thing called capacity. You may just need a rest day, and that's okay!) If we allow ourselves to listen to the little deceptions that are justifications, we keep digging ourselves a hole and burying ourselves.

Well Chris, this is all great, but how do I change? Some people are naturally SA, but I am not. I'm going to give you questions to ask yourself as well as habits to create to discover the "where you are" part of this exercise. One thing to do frequently is revert to your toddler self. Ask why. Ask why about everything! Why are you doing this or that? I don't mean what is the result but what is the purpose, what is in your heart? Get to the root. Don't settle for the surface thoughts, but find the true reason buried in your heart. Until you challenge yourself and ask honestly and get to the heart of these thoughts and actions, you'll always be in this hole, and bring people down in there with you.

Are you tithing 10% to the church just because you are supposed to, like another bill, or do you give it as an opportunity to give and serve? Did you help that person so that one day you could get a favor back, or because you saw someone in need and had the resources to help? Did you do an act simply for praise? Are you having a kid because you think it will help your marriage? Are you drinking alcohol just to be social or are you drowning some sorrows?

Yeah, I took a deeper turn at the end. Life is messy and we all make some wrong turns for right and wrong reasons. I'm trying to be direct and tackle the hard things. I am not writing this book to be a generic self-help book with general concepts or ideas to give people a false sense of accomplishment. I'm writing to be a true catalyst for change in lives where possible. I usually don't like direct challenge, questioning, or "called out" where it happens, but it ultimately is good to have it brought to the surface and addressed

Recently, in the book *Mindset: The New Psychology of Success* by Carol Dweck, I learned some new principles I was unaware of. There are those that have a fixed mindset and those that are open mindset; a mind is like a parachute; it only works when it's open. Granted, I knew this already. What I didn't realize was how a (closed) fixed mindset could operate. The over simplified version states that a fixed mindset is, "I have what I have, and I know what I know. I can't become any more or greater."

These folks may have some great talent naturally, but don't deal well with failure. Having failed at something, they equate themselves as a failure. Not having the ability to grow would be a stress I couldn't imagine. Knowing I can get better motivates me when I'm struggling. Dweck tells of how a kid in her class came to tears as she was teaching the concept. The poor guy thought that all he had was all he would ever have, and that he would never be good enough! If you are someone that constantly doesn't feel you are good enough or could never be more than you are, you need to read Dweck's book. Seriously. Go ahead; stop reading mine for a moment, order hers, and get back to this one!

Beyond consistently asking yourself "why," I want you to talk to yourself. I mean a purposeful conversation. Not the anxiety ridden why did I say that? Like when the cashier says drive safe and your response is "you too" and there's that awkward oops and then stumble away.

It's important that we put time aside from the day to day circus of life and have a true introspective conversation with ourselves. Have you recently discovered what you truly want in this current season of life? What gifts do you have and can take advantage of? Is there something you have been wanting to do and haven't attempted yet? Why? Is it resources, which can be retrieved, gained, or manifested? Is it fear of success or failure? Do you not have the skill to do what you are inspired to do? *Get out of that fixed mindset!*

Bill Gates didn't always know how to do what he now does. He learned and grew into it. I didn't know how to write a book. I took some action steps. I put it together as I went. Along the way, I found people who have written a book and received guidance. Resources can always be found and dug up. Decisions and actions are always on you.

One of the concepts I'm working on with myself right now is talking to myself about the real deep things. There are some generational problems in my family that I have decided is stopping with me. The only way this can happen is if I address it. Talk to myself about it. Become aware of these problems. Talk to my mom about it. Talk to my brother.

There are so many broken and unhealed people out there. Chances are, you are one of them. Usually it is because people don't talk and connect. If they do, it's just on the surface and not heart to heart. A person can have one thousand Facebook and Instagram followers and not one person to call for help. We all crave true connection and generally seek it where it is safe. That could be an unhealthy relationship or an inanimate object.

What happens when that connection is never found? Every other week, we hear of a presumed happy and successful person tragically killing themselves. Why? I personally believe it is isolation. Not only is it possible to be surrounded by people yet still feel alone, but it is happening and is rampant!

If you are battling something and haven't talked to anyone, there is a good chance if you start with your family, one of them has been dealing with the same thing. Alcohol, anger, the inability to connect to a significant other, etc., can all have generational ties. I'm asking you to face yourself and find out what it is that has been tripping you every step of the way, if it's past hurts or current hurdles. Talk to a family member or close friend openly and honestly. If the first person doesn't relate or is flippant about it, seek someone else. We weren't designed to do life alone, so quit trying to do it that way.

Now that you have made a conscious conversation, it's time to look at what you say to yourself internally and externally that isn't conducive. You reap what you sow. You can't plant carrot seeds and expect sweet potatoes. What words (seeds) are you sowing? Your reality is usually a mirror of your expectations. What unnecessary words and thoughts are you allowing to run on repeat? I have few that I say or think without meaning to; "I'm nervous," "Bet that isn't going to work," "Here we go again." It's these little jabs at yourself that will delay, hinder, or altogether kill your joy.

Here's an example of how to kill your day every day. It's inevitable that someone is going to ask you how your day is. When your response is something like mine used to be, you're sucking the wind out of your sails instead of filling them. It's a "Could be better, could be worse," mentality. Well, my days were going like that. Things could always get worse, but the worst part was they could've always been better. I was capping how high I could go. Now, my response is, "I am excellent," with the proper energy to go with it. Hard to be down when you act like you're not! Please start to be present and aware that you are stealing the wind out of your own sails and correct it with a positive thought or out loud word about the situation. Even repeat it a few times. With some consistency the negatives might not go away 100%, but you will be stepping in the right direction.

A couple of weeks ago I went to the grocery store. The cashier lady was friendly. I don't know how, though. In less than 3 minutes she managed to start 4 or 5 different sentences that began with, "I hate." I don't know how anyone can keep that up for any extended period of time and not feel crushed in their soul! If this describes you, perhaps a shower will help.

Your body needs a shower, do you not realize your brain needs one too? More than once a day, too! IN FACT, science says it takes about 5 positive thoughts or comments to erase every negative one. If you are calling yourself whatever negative word in the book 10 times a day, are you getting the 50 positive words to counteract it? I doubt it. Why not get rid of the negatives and increase the positives to get out of debit in the positive bank? Motivational videos, self-talk, actions moving toward your goal, putting yourself in the fellowship of good people, etc., is your brain shower.

You won't accidentally get this cleansing. When you shower at home, you need to have prepared first. You need the soap and washcloth or fluffy ball thing. You also need soap, shampoo, conditioner, skin products, etc. If you're like me, bald, some of those are erroneous. You hopefully have gotten yourself a towel to dry off. Showering your mind is going to take preparation, too. You don't just shower every now and again, right? You don't wait till you look like Pigpen from Peanuts to get a shower. You don't wait until you smell to get a shower. Why wait until the negative things hit to shower your mind? In the morning you can have any number of videos playing in the background. I guarantee you that if you listen to motivational videos from the time you roll out of bed to at least an hour or two later, you will notice a good difference in your life. *Yes, even over the weekend.*

If you do or have done this, you know the benefit. If you haven't, does that sound like a waste to you? Does that sound too uncomfortable? Sound like something that is too much effort? Well, let me ask you another question. Who and where were you 2, 5, and 10 years ago? Would you go back to being that person? Are you where you thought you would be today as of 2, 5, and 10 years ago? If you would prefer to go back to that person, you've been moving backward, and you need the positive reinforcement. If you are not where you thought you would be yet, maybe the extra motivation and positive conscious/subconscious reinforcement would help you move further along.

I'd like to add a recent testimony to this practice. I conducted an inadvertent field study on myself. For 3 to 5 weeks I had stopped listening to the positive speeches and interviews I normally kept on during the mornings. I was listening to educational topics instead. I figured it was still some organic brain food. I'm still doing myself some good. *WROOOONNNGGG!*

Over the last week or so I noticed my mood, self-talk, and outlook on things had taken an abrupt downturn. I kept letting my writing get sidetracked. As I said in the intro, I haven't mastered everything I am putting in this book and when I think I have, that's when I am really moving backward. I am making mistakes and growing right alongside you. Each day I am susceptible to the same laws of this world and human body you are. Know that you aren't getting it 100% "right" most days and you aren't the only one.

Enough about us for a moment, though. Let's go back to what Derpy didn't realize in the beginning; that all external vision comes from inside you. Your eyes see it, your mind processes it, then your mind's eye reflects it how you see it. That processing is computed with the same pathways you go to mostly. Your brain physically has pathways of processing thoughts. How you see and process the external world will become consistent. If that consistency isn't positive or is snap reacting without being present, that is the habit you'll fall into operating in. That is a fall we all too often make that results in hitting many branches on the way down.

As you can tell, I like to define things. It gets everyone singing from the same page. Let's define the words "act" and "react" to compare them.

Act - Take action, do something; Behave in the way specified

React - Respond or behave in a particular way in response to something; Respond with hostility opposition, or a contrary course of reaction to.

If you are constantly reacting, you are not in control of your life. Someone else always is. If you've never heard that before, take a second to think about it. Raise your hand if you want to be a puppet.

I didn't think so.

Every time you let yourself get angry and react instead of becoming present and aware, that is what you're doing. A little secret is that this doesn't just apply to other people. Raise your hand if you want to be the puppet of an inanimate object? I *definitely* didn't think so.

Let's give you an example of this inanimate object. My first winter up north I learned a few things I never had to deal with in the south. The major one was that salt gets on your windshield and if you use your wipers, it creates a sheen on the windshield, and you become blinded when driving into the sun. I knew there was a car in the left lane and none to my right. I did my best to just stay straight, maybe a smidge to the right to err on the side of caution. Well, in this spot, there was a curb that jutted out. I broke one rim, bent the other, and popped two tires.

I had two options. Let myself lose control or stay aware in the moment. I decided to stay aware. I took note that no one got killed, which was very possible. I could have ended up with a totaled car. Instead, I just had a situation that was a nuisance and was going to cost me a little money. Money that I didn't have, but it was what it was. I formulated a plan and got it done. I didn't let this inanimate object and situation rule me. Put a win down for Chris that day. I had another day, a couple of years previously, when changing a fuel pump I found myself reacting with choice words. You win some, you lose some.

Be it due to emotions, lack of presence at the moment, lack of maturity, or lack of self-awareness, some people have trouble maintaining their composure. The tail isn't supposed to wag the dog. Work towards making it less often where how you feel dictates what you do. A "Derpy" is going to let themselves go to a McDonalds and get irate in the line for something out of their control. Then they'll follow up with a silly action like calling 911 or ending up in a video online with a brawl in the McDonalds. In the grand scheme of things, that little situation is maybe embarrassing and then over. Let that same person run a company and have to work with managers, clients, vendors, etc., and they'll struggle.

The words self-awareness can be misleading. This may not be you, but we often get caught up in ourselves. I know I do. As early as I could remember, I decided that I only had myself to depend on. That's not entirely true, I had good friends along the way, but the damage I received from early youth had been done. I will tell people easily what I went through. I do, however, have a real hard time truly connecting. I am very introspective. This has increased my level of SA. However, for ANYONE to reach higher levels of SA, you have to have others for a fresh perspective. That's how the word self-awareness is misleading.

To truly and in an ongoing manner be self-aware, you need to seek counsel from good and wise counsel that wants to see you do and be better. You have blind spots. Believe as hard as you want that you know everything about yourself. You are with yourself 24/7 so you should know yourself best, right? Wrong. #fakenews.

We look at everything in life through our own prisms of thought and belief. Those thoughts and beliefs are sometimes on false foundations. Through having an open discussion with good insightful mentors, you will be able to see your blind spots. Additionally, seeing something every day makes it harder to see the whole forest. I was just in a client's building this week and pointed out an item that was in a precarious position. "Oh, I didn't realize that was there," was his response. It's HIS building and he didn't see it. To up your SA game, you are going to want to recruit one or more trusted advisors.

Because this book is mostly based on a lot of inspection of the self, I don't bring up interaction with others too much. This seems like a good spot to add this important nugget of info. It's been said that you can determine who you are as a person by taking your 6 closest friends and averaging them. In less scientific terms, "If you lay down with dogs, you get fleas."

Another adage I heard was you want to put yourself in the vicinity of those that are "better" than you. For example, if your goal is to play basketball better, are you going to play a game with Michael Jordan or Michael the next-door neighbor? I was recently introduced to an example that helps illustrate this. Iron sharpens iron. You may have heard that before. Let's run this thought out further. Take an iron axe. It's the sharpest it's ever been. Whack it into a tree and over time you get a dull axe and a tree with some damage.

Don't be an axe and pair yourself with a piece of wood. One will end up dull and the other hurt. This could be a business relationship where partners are unequal in their goals or a romantic relationship way out of balance on values and life outlook. I'm not saying because you are "better" than someone in a particular area, now they're the wood and you're the axe. Just make sure you and the people you surround yourself with are sharpening each other. The relationship that pulled me from Georgia to New Jersey had an extremely glass half empty outlook. I am almost polar opposite. We were not sharpening each other.

Speaking of looking at the world as a glass half empty— As of this writing, I've been in NJ for almost 3 years. When I first moved up, I got the "Why would you move here?" question. Usually the accompanying facial expression was that of a baby eating a lemon for the first time.

Then there was the usual follow up question, "Which is better; Savannah, Ga or Jersey?"

I answered that question a few different ways at first, but I have settled on these two metaphors. The first is that it is cakes and pies. You don't compare a perfectly made red velvet cake to an awesome blueberry pie with a tasty dollop of cool whip. They both are awesome, just two different experiences. During the follow up, I use it as a teaching moment. I tell folks that there are people where if you put them in Heaven, they would find something to complain about. I am not one of those people. Human nature is to try and find the imperfections, though.

Imagine, for a moment, a coin with a perfectly shiny newly minted side. The other side, though, is marred and scarred. Our culture and human nature is to look at that coin and focus on how horribly marred and scarred it is. But if you just flip that coin over, you have a brilliant beautiful coin. With that concept, please realize this; with everything in life there is going to be "good" and "bad". Winning the lottery has ups and downs. Each day we have the opportunity to focus on one and acknowledge the other. We typically acknowledge the good, flip the coin over and focus on the bad. I am asking you to, each day, make the conscious effort to reverse that habit. Hence the title of the book, Flip the Coin!

Find the silver lining in those bad things. Focus on the good and acknowledge the bad. I am not asking you to live in a land of delusion. I'm asking you to learn to dedicate your time and efforts on what is going to bring you forward in life, instead of derailing it with constant negativity.

I heard a great story one time that I want to share to challenge this idea of good and bad. There was this man that had a horse and the horse ran away. His neighbor came over and heard the news and said "oh, that's so bad. Sorry to hear that." The man says " good or bad, who am I to say?" A day later the horse comes back and brings another one with it. The neighbors' response? " That's good, you have a new horse. The man says " good or bad, who am I to say?" The next day his son breaks a leg while trying to train the new horse. The neighbor says what we would think "oh that's bad." Of course the old man is unflinching and still believes " good or bad, who am I to say?" The next day the government comes to draft his son to war but of course with the broken leg, he can't go. So, we do have to be cautionary on what we ascribe to being good or bad and sometimes we will only know in retrospect.

The reason the flip the coin concept is in the Self-Awareness chapter is we do this negative focus often. To give an example, I'll point to a person I knew. We'll call her Tracy. Tracy liked to say she was realistic. Tracy knew she wasn't a glass half full person, but she wasn't aware of just how negative she was and how it affected her. She commonly would not put herself in the shoes of the other person to see their point of view. She would complain about how other people were negative, but then turn around and be just as negative herself. Just to be clear and fair here, she had some great qualities and ultimately a good heart. We just were not a good match and these were some of the characteristics that were a wedge for us. Nor was I perfect and I had plenty of blind spots and deficiencies I have made some progress on. I can't beat her up and make me out to be perfect, that was not the case.

Back to the point though, this was draining to her. She physically got ill often. It is known that the body will physically manifest our constant negative feelings. Since we were close, this brought me down as well. Once we separated, I could have looked at all the "bad" that had happened. I had failed at a relationship. I moved away from my friends and family and was in a state with almost no one in my corner. I didn't have many resources at my disposal. I could have let that be my focus and slid into "woe is me" depression.

The other option was to acknowledge that those things were real. I was quite aware of that. However, there were some other very real things to notice, too. I am living in an area with tons of opportunities. There are some experiences to be had that I can only get here in this area. I've had some tremendously awesome experiences already from having moved. My eyes are open to things I didn't know before. I've stretched far beyond what I thought I was capable of. I could go on, but that is what I focused on. Moving forward! I'm asking you to become SA to notice what you never knew about yourself. Look at what habits you have. Not just at what you do, but how you think. There are tons of decisions you make without thinking about them, and if you become aware, you could drastically change your life!

This is important not just for what you get out of life, but also how you enjoy it. Your mind and body are connected. As I said, Tracy got ill a lot! Plans I made got cancelled because she didn't feel good the day of. Plans she made got cancelled a lot as well. She let herself pre-stress things that were coming. She let herself puff things up to being larger than they were. You can have everything you need and literally think yourself into depression, anxiety, stomach problems, even DEATH! The good news? You can think your way out of those. Well, maybe not death. If you stressed yourself into a heart attack and ended up in a casket or the crematorium, you're not coming back from that. You get the point though.

There's another thing to be learned from Tracy. In today's society, this is a huge problem and it isn't just me picking on her. This problem is quite rampant in our society and being exacerbated by social media: self-love. Tracy would get mad that I didn't compliment her but every time I did, she turned it negative. Of course, I eventually stopped. I was tired of her putting herself down. I'd listen to and watch her beat herself up in the mirror. If someone we knew was being verbally attacked, hopefully we could bring ourselves to step in and help. What do you do when it is herself beating herself up?

Free slightly off topic advice; no one likes watching their partner beat themselves up. Especially when you're beating yourself up for something you could change, but don't, or beating yourself up for something you can't do anything about. Tracy certainly had her complications in life that led to that state. I am not condescendingly pointing this out, it's just an observation. I have my own self-love things that I am working on, like anybody else. Anyway, I'm going to ask you to love and care for yourself so much that you don't leave yourself where you are. Pick up on the parts and pieces of this book that can help you move forward and develop more self-love.

Wrap up items

ooo Don't fool yourself

We lie to ourselves so much! I'll remember to do ___ when I get home. Tomorrow I'll actually start XXXXX habit. Tomorrow I'll stop XXXXXX habit.

Well, those are a few examples of me fooling myself. Especially that "I'll remember" one. It's very easy to say we will be a different person tomorrow. Tomorrow for some reason never gets here. Sacrifice the person you are today so you can be the person you need to be tomorrow. This is important so I am going to repeat it. Sacrifice the person you are today, so you can be the person you need to be tomorrow.

ooo How to avoid a multi car pile-up in your life

It's common for a conflict to escalate. The problem gets exaggerated. Emotions get exaggerated. The situation can really get out of hand. How do we avoid this? The same way getting involved in a vehicle pile-up is avoided.

The training for a driving job involves a formula. Space + Vision = Time. While driving down the road, avoid clumping yourself into a group of cars. That's space. Keep your eyes scanning the road ahead and behind. That is vision. With those two pieces in place, barring crazy circumstances, you have time to act in accordance with the situation. Take either space or vision away and now you are stuck reacting to the situation. Huge difference. The same is how you go about your daily challenges. If you don't have self-awareness and presence, you're just meandering through your life.

ooo Giving credibility to your struggles

Matthew McConaughey has come quite far from *Alright, Alright, Alright*. He has a very awesome speech that he gave at a college graduation. I highly recommend you spend the 45 minutes listening to it at some point. Because I always think I can be and do better, I sometimes beat myself up too much. "If I had only done this," or "That is better," is something I've thought or said quite often. What I have learned to do is give credibility to the struggles.

There are some very daunting challenges I have put myself into. Some I've done great and some I've been a fish out of water. Those times when I didn't do so well hit my self-esteem instead of realizing I tried. I stepped out of my comfort zone. I did something that possibly a huge percentage of people wouldn't have tried.

If you are one of those people like me that doesn't give credibility to your mountains, you are in for a world of hurt. Self-doubt, crushing pressure, never a sense of accomplishment, and other negative side effects can result. Give some credibility to the hurdles. Learn to be joyful and happy where you are and with your shortcomings, but don't live there. Keep moving gleefully knowing you are moving forward.

ooo Seek counsel to get out of the trees

I grew up in Savannah, Georgia. I never hunted until one day a newer friend said to me, "Look at this."

He took me to his freezer in the garage and it was fully loaded with meat. He showed me the prices, and well, a hunter was born. This led to me doing something I never had to do before; go out in the woods and not get lost. I quickly learned the woods at day and at night were two different animals. One early morning, while still dark, I was heading out to my tree stand. I was lost until day light trying to figure out where the tree was that I was looking for. I started off close, but the more I searched the further away I ultimately ended up!

I bring this up because life is like this. I have written on looking inside yourself for answers. Question yourself to get to the root thoughts and ideas. Equally important is to look outside for answers. Genesis chapter 2 verse 18. *It is not good for man to be alone.* This isn't quite the context it was written about, but still applies. The wisest of men and women seek counsel. They know and are aware of their limitations of knowledge and their blind spots. We all need counsel in various ways.

ooo Become a stripper

Not really, but metaphorically. The bottom line of all this SA chapter, and this entire book really, is to be a stripper. Strip off all of the extra weights slowing us down. We can't get rid of them if we don't know they are there. We can't get rid of these weights if we don't perceive them as weights.

Hebrews 12:1 - *Therefore, since we are surrounded by such a huge crowd of witnesses to the life of faith, let us strip off every weight that slows us down, especially the sin that so easily trips us up. And let us run with endurance the race God has set before us.* The author doesn't say let us strip off our sins.

He says let us strip off the weight that slows us down, especially sin. That means we are not supposed to only question if it is a sin or not, but rather is it good for us or not. The thoughts and tools in this book, when boiled down, is to help you to strip off the weights of what is not good. The distractions of the world. Hindering feelings and emotions. The people who seek only to take and never contribute. The false perspectives we live in. Lies we tell ourselves. As this chapter is concerned specifically, not being aware of yourself and your thoughts lead to non-conductive thoughts or actions in your life.

○○● Avoiding (growing) pain

When you do what is hard, usually in the long run life will be easier. There are millions of examples of this we can see through history and present day. However, we work so hard at avoiding pain. Avoiding discomfort. The problem with this broken thinking? Pain is unavoidable. Don't let yourself experience the pain of the gym or delayed gratification of food? Enjoy your heart disease, or if you are being chased by a bear, you'll most likely be the slowest.

Try as hard as you might, pain is going to find you. Listen to the story of David Goggins. His story is amazing, and the amount of sheer will he has developed is out of this world! He's done Hell Week 3 times, ran an insane number of miles in 24 hours, and has the world record for pull ups. He has incredible mind control. He says when he is training for these items, he isn't really training for those events. He is training for that call at 3 A.M. that his mom is dead. He is training his mind to be calloused and resilient to the pain in life.

It's coming. Instead of avoiding it, run towards it like a crazed masochist and learn how to be fruitful in it! Maybe that was a bit of an overstatement, but you get the picture. Spend too much time avoiding pain and you cut a neural pathway for it. We've all heard "no pain, no gain". Generally, that phrase is right. I noticed the other day that I had made a habit of doing only four of the 6 different exercises each morning. In the grand scheme of things, that is a small change. In the long run I lose a lot of dividends from my exercises. Worst though, is that I mentally start to let myself shortcut in that small area and find myself shortcutting other areas that will cost me in the long run.

ooo Sticky like a freshly burnt marshmallow (now I want smores, and none in the house).

You've got to have some stickability. This relates a bit to the pain concept before here. Stick to the decisions made in a good mood when it is long gone. In some cases, it's vice-versa. "That's the last time I do tequila shots", until next Saturday.

It's easy to say "I'm going to be more kind" but hard to follow up.. This session of writing right now is the result of telling myself that this was my writing day. I have lots of things I would find more enjoyable at the moment. Realistically, none of it would be fruitful or pay future me any dividends. This book is meant to pay me dividends. Not just the cash I'm shooting to earn. My goal in life is to help others achieve more. I must, right now, do what I don't feel like, to be in-purpose on-purpose and also later I can better enjoy doing what I want.

ooo Cut the fat

I don't mean that succulent bit on a perfectly cooked steak. I mean in your life. One of the best ways to be more, is to be less! Over a few months I've made small changes that have made a huge and helpful difference. Cutting the TV. Cutting the music. Cutting the distractions that kept me back. I have a ton of shows I would love to watch and keep up with. For some reason when I was watching these shows, I felt I would be missing something if I stopped. My curious mind of needing to know how things wrap up is part of it.

I watch much less TV and movies now. You know what's funny? My world is still spinning. In fact, it's better. If I really wanted to know what was going on in the show, I could always google it. However, it didn't change my life negatively like I had some weird feeling it would. What do I do with this time? Invest it into productivity. The need-to and want-to's. Being in-purpose on-purpose has its own enjoyment!

ooo Big wall or small wall?

I put in this chapter earlier the lady that said, "I hate," rapid fire about different items. This is how we block ourselves consistently. Maybe you are thinking, "I never say that word." This thought still applies to you. We make things so much bigger than they are.

Let me explain. Imagine you draw a 9 on the ground. Someone comes up, sees the 9 upsides down, and claims it's a 6. This could be a friend or enemy and y'all can still stand there arguing for hours. If you two stand side by side and look at the number, though, you'll agree. It's about perspective, right?

So, how about that situation on the road where you got cut off. Maybe someone took "your" parking spot. Someone at the office got the last bit of coffee and didn't make anymore. Someone else trickled work to you and you didn't have enough coffee for it. You go to the store on the way home needing your favorite vice to reward yourself for making through such a tough day. They're sold out. Along the day you thought or said out loud to yourself "I hate," or "I can't stand," or "this always happens to me,", etc.

The problem here is you are setting a precedent of a negative and overwhelmed mindset and feeling. The real tragedy is these problems are so small in the reality of your life and day. In all of these situations, if you became present and called the situation what it is, a minor impedance, you can let it go (If you're a parent and seen Frozen, you're now singing).

So, let's rework this day. You got cut off while driving. But did you die? Was there any harm? Or, was it simply a nuisance? Perhaps that person is having a much worse or better day. They're trying to get to the hospital where their wife is in labor or a family member is dying. Maybe, maybe not. Either way, it's a nuisance that is going to happen. If you don't like it, don't drive. Now that we've let that go, we aren't driving angry the rest of the way to work and our anger tank is still empty.

Now take this thinking through the rest of the day. No more coffee! Well, I can put a pot on and go through my emails or to the restroom while it brews. Life goes on and no one is hurt. You're handed more work that is someone else's fault. Legitimate frustration. See if there is a way to discover a root cause and fix it. If not, you have two options;

keep that job or don't. Is it worth quitting or worth giving up control of yourself by letting someone else control your emotions and reactions? This all sounds obvious as I type it, but as of last week I had a day where I let stress get the best of me. As I said at the beginning of the book, I am progressing just like any other human.

For the lesson here, I want you to start defining things as they truly are, not as what you think or feel like they are. To get you started, let's define some of these feelings and emotions we think we know and start to understand them a little more. Definitions provided by dictionary.com.

Hate – to dislike intensely or passionately; feel extreme aversion for or extreme hostility toward; detest:

Vexed – irritated; annoyed

Inconvenient – not easily accessible or at hand: inopportune; untimely: not suiting one's needs or purposes

Happy – delighted, pleased, or glad, as over a particular thing

Joy – a source or cause of keen pleasure or delight; something or someone greatly valued or appreciated:

Anger – a strong feeling of displeasure and belligerence aroused by a wrong; wrath; ire

Impede – to retard in movement or progress by means of obstacles or hindrances; obstruct; hinder.

Simple inconvenience here and there can add up if we make a big deal. We let multiple accounts of this collect through our week and before we know it, we're living unhappily. Keep aware of these little situations so they don't add up.

ooo **The wall or your head, which is harder?**

This goes without saying but needs to be brought up. Mistakes are not always obvious. For example, as positive as I try to always be, I had my previous issue with grumbling. It took me longer than it should have to figure out I was in a poor attitude loop and fix it.

Be vigilant at finding the mistakes in your mentality, energy, actions, and life. Missteps are going to happen. It's the mistakes you repeat that hurt the most. Vigilantly look for these mistakes and places for improvement. Also, just because we "fixed" something once, doesn't mean it's forever fixed.

ooo **Knowing isn't always knowing, know what I mean?**

We have all done it. We thought we knew what the person we were talking to was about to say. There have been a few times I've been in this situation and I wasn't wrong, but I wasn't fully right either. They added to what I knew so then I knew more. It is important to be aware of these four situations.

1. Knowing what you know.
2. Learning what you don't know.
3. Not knowing what you know.
4. Not learning what you don't know.

I am 100% sure there are many concepts, ideas, or thoughts you've read in this book that aren't new. Maybe illustrated in a different way, but not new. I also am quite sure there are some items in this book you have never heard of. Sometimes I get a little self-righteous and think I know more than I do. Then I have to get a reality check and realize I don't know what I don't know. That's where reading and mentorship is important. We were not created to get through this world alone. We have to set our ego aside and reflect on situations with the four scenarios above.

Chapter 3

"What Direction Am I In?" Formulas

"Success is walking from failure to failure without the loss of enthusiasm." - Winston Churchill

There's a formula out there Linkin Park fans probably know of, courtesy of Fort Minor's own Mike Shinoda:

The Name Formula
10% luck + 20% skill + 15% concentrated power of will + 5% pleasure + 50% pain = 100% reason to remember the name.

It's a great song, but it doesn't incite much reflection on where you are and where you're going in life. While it gives you a beat to move to, there are no tools to move in the direction you're shooting for. So, with that in mind, I created a slightly more complex, but also more useful, formula to live by: It seems like a lot at first, but bear with me. Like I said in the beginning, this book is for you to take what works for you and leave the rest. I hope this section makes sense to you and is useful. If it isn't, read through to take it in and leave it behind.

Growth Formula
$$(Energy(Purpose + How) \times Action)^{Time + Focus} = Growth$$

Your **Positive Energy** multiplied by a **Purpose** and **Plan** (the "how" in this case) is then multiplied by your chosen **Action**. This result is exponentially affected by the amount of **Time** plus **Focus** you've devoted. This equals **Growth.**

Stagnation Formula
$$(-Energy(Apathy + Excuses) \times Procrastination)^{Time + Distraction} = Stagnation$$

Your **Negative Energy** multiplied by **Apathy** and **Excuses** is then multiplied by **Procrastination.** This result is exponentially affected by the amount of **Time** plus **Distraction** you've spent. This equals **Stagnation.**

These formulas are designed to give you a macro and micro tool. On the macro side, it can help you see the whole forest of your life and create a visual of where you are and going. On the micro side, it can help you see what trees in your forest you need to prune or fertilize.

Here is why this formula is important: have you ever been driving in a hilly area and you aren't sure if you are climbing in altitude or decreasing? Airplanes have an instrument that helps with this. It's called an Attitude Indicator— NOT "altitude", but "attitude". When I learned the name, I loved how serendipitous it was to be called that.

When you get going through life and decide to make some changes and really buckle down, generally, you won't see the fruit of your efforts right away. It can become quite disheartening. Imagine you've had a garden for 3 months, 9 months, 2 years, and so forth, but did a poor job taking care of it or choosing the best soil. It will take time to improve your garden and reverse the damage of neglect or poor-quality care.

In the same way, you have built up certain ways of thinking, acting, and speaking. It will take some concentrated time of better thoughts, words, and actions to really improve where you are. Utilizing the above formulas, you can figure out important details on a large scale. Use this to create a vision for the future and grow towards it. It's important to note that you won't have everything in life or about yourself figured out and that is okay. Most often the most successful people have glimpses of a vision that they continuously move toward, filling the blanks as they go. If you wait until you know the whole story, you'll never stop waiting.

I recently heard a really great thought about vision I want to share before I go any further. There is a difference between vision and a good idea. A vision you will sacrifice for. Make time for it. It will be a part of you. A good idea is, well, just a good idea. If it isn't a part of your DNA and make-up like a true vision, it may not be worth your time and that is okay.

Back to the formula, on a smaller day-to-day scale, this formula will help you figure out where you are on your path. This is important because even when it feels like you are not going anywhere, as long as you can check the boxes, you can tell you are growing. If there's resistance, it's not necessarily a bad thing. Like a car going uphill, sometimes you just need a bit of extra power before enjoying the easier roll down.

Also important, however, is figuring out the small items you are missing. Water boils at 212 °F, not 211 °F. Often folks are just missing that one degree and give up too soon. The complication with success and failure is that they can look like one another.

In Tulsa, Oklahoma there is a church by the name of Transformation Church. The pastor preached a series titled *Under Not Over*. In the first sermon he teaches the idea of *Planted, Not Buried*. In this illustration he notes that if you take a seed and stick it in the ground, then cover it with dirt, it is planted. If you take a dead body and stick it in the ground, then cover it with dirt, it is buried. The complication is that they look the same. There can be a massive root structure below, but until there's a sprout, it still looks the same for a time. Then, finally, after enough water and fertilizer (aka enough crap) the plant grows. The process of success and failure are usually both painstakingly slow processes.

When you're in the woods it is hard to see the whole forest. That is what this chapter is for, to look at your journey of success in bite sized pieces to see where you are excelling and where you are one degree away from boiling. The goal is to help you stop looking at one or two trees and instead come out of the forest to see the whole thing. As Jordan Peterson has said, "If you put off changing what makes you happy, then you're more miserable AND older."

Peterson is great at making life decisions more rational and less emotional. Let's point out some rational thoughts in this chapter and start moving forward.

The first thing I want to tackle is the simplest part. There is not an in-between of moving forward or moving backward. Water can be stagnant. Air can be stagnant. There is a caveat. You can't chop a tree down with a blunt axe. Taking necessary rest time to sharpen your axe is not considered being stagnant. If you are stagnant, then that is a lost opportunity at moving forward. Atrophy is not a place you want to live in!

Living in success doesn't mean you won't fail. Living in success means you move from failure to failure without loss of motivation. To learn and improve you must make mistakes. The quicker you experience the failures, the sooner you are prepared for that "lucky" opportunity that is coming your way. In life, there are those moments of "pure luck". This isn't actually what we tend to perceive it as, however. It is preparation from lots and lots of activity and mistakes. When what you learned from those mistakes crosses with opportunity, you have "luck".

If I told you 57.5 mistakes is all that lies between you and 1 million dollars, how rapidly would you make those mistakes? I'm telling you now that everyone has X amount of mistakes between them and their goals. The catch is that you can't just make the mistake and move to the next one without ever changing. You find what lesson is in the mistake and then gleefully move on to apply it to the next one!

A common theory is that it takes 10,000 hours to master a skill or craft. What most people don't realize, though, is that one hour every now and again will not work. It takes hours chained together. The tighter you pack them hours in, the easier it is to learn from mistakes and build muscle memory. On my wall I have a picture to keep me mindful of this. It says, "If not us, who and if not now, when?"

Remember to give the struggles you face some credibility. They are your struggles. If you chalk up your successes to merely luck, you have cheated yourself of a needed victory to re-energize and reinvigorate yourself. Take the victory to keep moving forward with enthusiasm!

The next component I want to point out is time. It's always there, one of the few things in life that is predictable and never failing. The seconds will always tick on by at the same rate every day. Time can't be saved. It can only be spent. While I won't say deny yourself fun and experience for your entire life, I will say it won't kill you to delay some gratification.

Marry your time to focus. All day, every day. You have to be vigilant and wise with your time. You don't want to be an arrow randomly pulled from the quiver and thrusted just anywhere through the air, right? Maybe you are still figuring out what your purpose in life is. That's okay. Your goals don't have to be just profession based. There are plenty of other personal items you need to work on before, during, and after figuring out what your purpose is. However, don't let yourself get struck by the fear of lost time or creeping death. It's all about balance.

In my health class in 9th grade I was learning from my not-so-healthy looking teacher. One of the concepts we learned was creeping obesity. He told us that was what had happened to him. It was explained as slowly gaining weight over time until you become obese without knowing how. One way to say it is "if you are not actively trying to be healthy, then you're actively trying to not be healthy."

Let's apply the same thought to your life's purpose. We don't all find out what our purpose is in a simple, "Ah-ha!" moment. Sometimes it is that thing that everyone else sees you are great at and it's easy to you but not most others. Sometimes it is that thing you think everyone else should do and can't figure out why they aren't. Sometimes we must work our way into purpose.

We do that by focusing on our God given talents and abilities and see where it leads us. Perhaps it isn't related to any talents or abilities and it is instead a passion, a drive, or something that has been stuck in our minds for as long as we can remember. If you're like me, you simply never intentionally moved that direction. All I saw on that path was hurdles, but any other direction led to nowhere. Creeping death is not moving in the direction of your purpose and can come in another form as well, when you've found your purpose but are letting yourself be sidetracked with distractions.

Distractions. TV, keeping up with the Jones, getting bogged down in the trivial, and I'm sure you could come up with a ton more. Not all distractions are bad. Kids, family, friends, the occasional vacation to recharge the batteries. All good things to have in life at the core, but they can all rob you of your potential successes if you let them. Balance is one of the more difficult skills in life to sharpen. Get creative at minimizing the distractions. Spend more time focused on the goals and building blocks of your future and less time going the wrong way. That last sentence is especially for me. I am really good at staying busy with something that needs to be done at some point, but may not actually be top priority for the moment.

I'm a visual person, so I'll illustrate a scenario. Let's pretend for a moment that you are in a busy city. It is 5:30 P.M. and the streets are jam-packed. You turn left instead of right at the intersection. The more time you spend in the wrong direction, the more it compounds against getting to your destination. Hence, time is an exponent in these formulas.

What effect does this have on you? Well, most likely, you were already not too happy about being in traffic. Now, because of your mistake, you are cursing yourself— or worse, everyone else who had nothing to do with it. Most likely you're now cutting off other cars, potentially causing wrecks, but you just kept going because you were so angry that you didn't care. You have spiraled right on out of control. (Déjà vu to that Self-Awareness chapter much?) Does that sound like someone you know, or the person in the mirror? It's always someone else's fault.

Equally as bad is constantly blaming and beating yourself up. There are plenty of others out there who will do that for you; don't do it to yourself. More often than not we know what is wrong. We know we aren't doing what we should. As Tony Robbins would say, turn those "shoulds" into "musts". He also jokes about how we "should" all over ourselves.

Every single time you don't do something you should, your conscious and/or subconscious remembers it. Then it compounds and compounds and compounds. Fast forward to anything going wrong and your mind will say, "Well, I knew I couldn't do it. You don't have what it takes to stick to anything. You'll never achieve that goal. You didn't deserve it anyway."

The problem is that you thought you couldn't, so you couldn't. That subconscious can be a real— well, the name for it wouldn't be considered nice words. Unless you program it to be an ally. That requires constant positive reinforcement. You've got to fight the natural programming to do things that are not comfortable. You've got to fight against the natural urge to avoid things we assign to be scary or a threat. Fight against the FEAR or get stuck living outside of your capabilities.

The beautiful phenomenon that happens with this repetition is that the uncomfortable becomes comfortable. Here is a tenet to living a successful life I hope to pass on; give 110% until you become comfortable with it and it becomes your new 100%. **Growth** starts at the first step you've never taken before. **Expansion** starts at pushing through what you thought was the last mile you could do! Disclaimer: we all have a thing called capacity. Yes we can expand and get a new 100% from growth. Also, we can only spend so much time growing. As I said before, rest and recharge is important, we are not machines!

One of the many keys to living a full life is to become comfortable being uncomfortable. No one is born tackling their dreams and goals, or anything for that matter, out of the womb. It's simply **GROWTH** and **EXPANSION**! Your objective should be to spend more time in this state of discomfort. It means you're trying new things and expanding more often than not. growing and harnessing your strengths. You have to have a PIONEERING MINDSET. Always look for and live in the new undiscovered territory of your mind, life, actions, efforts, and focus. Be the metaphorical Danny Boone of your own life. If you have to buy a

Danny Boone Crockett hat to stick on your wall to give you direct and subliminal messaging to be a pioneer, well, do what it takes.

Time to tie it all together with a big ol' pretty bow on this illustration and formulas. During the illustration, I asked how going the wrong way affected you. I detailed how you reacted and the fallout, but the initial answer was that you weren't too happy about it. Energy is MASSIVE! Energy is made up of enthusiasm/attitude, mentality/beliefs, and overall outlook. I have seen salespeople sell something they didn't believe in and excel. I've been the sales guy that totally believed in the product and wasn't doing good at getting it sold.

When we don't put the better energy into something, then the effort wasn't given a full chance. We then have ourselves a little self-fulfilling prophecy when it doesn't work out. The good news in this? We can start improving your energy today, with the little things. Don't eat that donut that was brought into work. It's a stinkin' ol' fast food donut anyway, not even a tasty mom and pop bakery donut that's worth the calories. Instead of the elevator, take the stairs. Park at the back of the parking lot. Go into work 5 minutes early and don't leave early. Listen to some good mood and positive mindset podcasts for 30 minutes while you get ready for the day. Speaking of, get up 20 minutes early and do 15 minutes of cardio. You get the picture.

Keep doing the tiny little things because you must, because later the compound of them will lead to what you truly want vs. doing what is easy because right now you'll not be burdened. The real benefit is the little, "Wow, I can do it!" compounded that will shift your mind to a whole better place. It's not the huge Hollywood moments that really make a difference (sorry-not-sorry to keep picking on you, Hollywood).

The defining moments are the daily small tiny decisions that you make, no matter how you feel. You still choose to do what will move you in the right direction. The more time spent there, the more exponential the effects on your life are!

Look at the success formula and think about your life. Each day, are you putting those pieces to work? The stagnation side is problems focused and the growth side is solutions focused. I hope it's not the wrong side of the scale you are most often embodying! Most folks say the purpose is the most important piece, because if you can get a strong enough purpose, you can figure out "the how". They're not wrong, but some of us just aren't going to figure out our purpose overnight. I have a few times over the years I thought I had. I had just borrowed some of the usual suspects (material things) and labeled that as my purpose.

If you put a purpose on your dream board and it doesn't motivate you or illicit an emotional response, you haven't discovered one of your real purposes yet. Fancy food, cars, and houses really do jack some people up enough, but it isn't enough for me. Today I had a meeting with a new client where I connected him to someone inside the industry. They are going to be able to refer and promote each other. I am also connecting him with a few other folks to assist in marketing, setting up E-commerce, and a few other connections. His business is going to rocket over the next one to three years, and while it's not because of me, I had some helping hand in it. Seeing how innovative and driven he is and knowing he is going to really make a difference in so many lives, I get charged up! That's part of my purpose!

Each day, I aim to make small and large differences in the lives of others that make life better for them and those around them. Just because it may sound noble, though, doesn't mean that you should do the same. If it doesn't grip you, don't make that your WHY. In a previous business life in my early 20's, I borrowed the dreams of others, including the cars, houses, vacations, and normal "dream" items people have. It wasn't enough to push me to be better, to do more, to think more, think larger. If you grab enough of the right goals, motivation won't be necessary. The inspiration will push you through!

ENERGY, positive or negative, is usually multiplied by what you give. This is important, so I am going to say it again; in life you get what you give, and usually multiplied! If you give off negative energy, you're almost certainly going to get it back and then some. It's the whole, "You get more bees with honey than vinegar" adage. A genuine positive and good attitude can make a ton of difference. You really have two choices in life: to be or not to be miserable. Misery loves company. If you choose to be happy no matter what, those miserable people will, over time, either disappear and leave you alone or become converts. Either way, you win.

There's a ton of folks I've heard say things along the lines of, "I'll be happy when I get (fill in the blank)". Either they almost never get what they wanted, or they do but the void doesn't get filled. If you can't figure out how to be happy and have gratitude now, chances are you won't be happy later when you get whatever "it" is. If you can't decide to be happy in the journey, it's generally not going to be found in its fullness at the destination.

If you think you have nothing else to offer the world, until you figure out what it really is that you have that can make a difference, let good energy be your contribution. If you have to fake it until you make it, do it. You might be waking up not quite happy or excited right this moment. Count your blessings that you have to be joyful and grateful over and put out good energy. A good energy and vibe can be the difference between being able to take advantage of an opportunity or not.

I can hear a few skeptics grumbling about me being mister glass half full, "Well, Chris, it's impossible to keep that good attitude through everything." There will be days where we miss the mark. When the struggles are large or back to back enough, even weeks at a time. We can't let it become the prevailing trend. Ask my friends and they'll tell you I'm usually Mister Positivity. When I told one of them that I was writing a book on positivity and growth, his response was that it makes perfect sense. To paraphrase, he said that I would find a way to make being gifted a crap sandwich have a silver lining. It may be hyperbole, but you get the point.

In that light, to be clear, I am not asking you to be blind or ignorant to reality or to look through rose-colored glasses all of the time. I feel bad, hurt, disappointed, unhappy, or any other of the lower ends of the spectrum of feelings like everyone else. I try to make sure I don't live there.

You can't go into a bad deal with a hopeful mind and good energy and expect it to be perfect. If you suffer a heart break, it is going to affect you. If you experience loss, it'll have its effect. You can control your perception, though. Maybe that person you loved isn't good for you and you're truly better off. Perhaps you get up and your car battery has quit holding charge and there is a meeting you have to be at by 10

A.M. but that meeting was in NYC on September 11th. Now that not working battery is no longer a source of stress, but a heaven-send.

What I am trying to portray in this concept is to not be ignorant or not feel the bad that can come with situations. However, don't let it rule your life! As a Southerner in the North, I learned the hard way not to run windshield wipers in the winter, because the salt smears and the sun makes it impossible to see through the windshield. The result was a cracked and bent rim and two popped tires. I was aggravated at first. Then I realized my car wasn't wrecked, no one got killed, and within about 2 hours I was going to have my car road worthy again. I could let it ruin my whole day or do what I had to and make the best of the rest of the day.

I've done a lot of explaining and gave a lot of opinions on the above concept. Hopefully it's been helpful in some way. That's not quite enough for me. Frankly, you're taking the time to read my book, so you deserve more impact than just a little helpful in some way. So, I have some questions for you.

Growth Formula
(Energy(Purpose + How) X Action)$^{\text{Time + Focus}}$ = Growth

Stagnation Formula
(-Energy(Apathy + Excuses) X Procrastination)$^{\text{Time + Distraction}}$ = Stagnation

When you look at the formulas side by side, what do you see? Are you spending more time moving forward or backward? When was the last time you really assessed yourself, your daily actions and thoughts? What habits, attitudes, thoughts, point of view, etc. are you going to inspect and challenge to change for the better? If you want something different, you've got to be different.

If there's something you've been wanting to do, but fear is holding you back, keep this thought close; the pain of not working toward your goal is more painful than the fear, I promise. I say that as a guy who has to push past this weird fear of making phone calls to expand business. Barring a disorder, we all experience fear. Feeling afraid doesn't make you a failure but living in it and not facing it does. We all procrastinate, at least from time to time, but it's only a failure if you let yourself live in it.

My goal with this chapter is to help you think about your decisions. The small daily choices that you make each day, those are the ones that really matter. If you can stop making the decisions based on a feeling or what's easier, you can focus on making choices that do more towards your goal. My advice is to slow down, become introspective, and think about those decisions.

Does your answer align with the success or the failure formula? It's going to take as much effort to fail as it is to succeed. "That doesn't make sense Chris," I hear you huff, but think of it this way: Eating healthy doesn't really take more time. Exercising 15 minutes a few days a week isn't that difficult to work in. Sitting in the hospital with the news that you have 3 blocked arteries, now that's real fear, real stress. Real work is dealing with that emotionally and financially. I'll work upfront and enjoy the benefits later!

We've all heard the stories that started with "Hold my beer and watch this," right? Usually something funny and a little painful is what follows. No good story starts with "Hold my milk." Well, no good success or underdog story starts with doing the least work possible. The true secret is that when you get a dream, inspiration, PURPOSE, the work and discomfort and sometimes pain seems worth it.

You're going to put in the work one way or another. Whether it's stressing being broke, doing something you don't want to, or both. You can play it safe and still fail or get hurt.

One of my thoughts I had about pain. Pain with a purpose hurts half as bad and pain without a purpose hurts twice as bad. Also, 86.37 percent of all statistics are made up. Kidding, but it's usually true that if we find purpose in it, it is more bearable. I'll use an easily understood example. Ask a woman to sign up for 9 months of discomfort followed with excruciating pain for no reason and she is going to decline. Ask her to do it for a baby, and many do. We could think, well, she didn't know what she was really signing up for on the pain and discomfort scale and it was blind confidence. I would agree if it wasn't for the fact of second and third born children. The purpose made it worth it and bearable.

Now I ask you how do you eat an elephant? Catch a whale? Make a mountain? I could continue but the point is simple enough. You start. You take the first bite. Take the first step. You just pick a place to start and start.

Dreams and visions are fantastic, but without action, they are just intangible ideas. That said, I'm not recommending you go all half-cocked toward your goals. It's very important to head towards them as calculated and intelligent as possible. That's where a plan and dates come in. With those plus some action, you have focus and a road map.

Imagine, for a minute, a ship heading out on a trip. It's leaving Fort Lauderdale, FL and is supposed to be going to St. Thomas in the

Caribbean. The further it travels in the wrong direction, the longer it takes to get to the Caribbeans when it finally gets corrected. Due to the delay, you now have some very ticked off cruisers. Hence, it's important to start off in the right direction rather than have to correct it later on, when possible.

Any person who has amassed success will tell you it is not a straight line. It is not going to be pretty. To make it easier on yourself, take the time to plan right. Use some reverse engineering. Get a clear vision of what you want and where you want to go. Put that goal down on paper with a realistic date. That will help you focus. Focusing in the right direction over time will make the difference. Most people overestimate what they can do in a year and underestimate what they can do in a decade, with some focus. Get this vision down on paper with a date. Visualize it as often as possible. Then walk it back to where you are currently. Make it bite size steps to help you stay on the path.

This book is a great example of this method in action. When I began, I put a date to have it published by. Walking it back, I had to figure out how to get it published; self-publish or a publishing company. This took some research, but I got "lucky" by putting the word out there that I needed information on this. Before I even finished half of the book, I had managed to get the publishing question answered. It was another step along the way to finishing the book, so that was under the goal and with a date. I missed the date I wanted to be done by. I did, however, finish and get it published. Without the goal and intentionality, it wouldn't have happened.

To make it more bite size, I jotted down thoughts and ideas for the book over time. In a couple short weeks, I had chapters and some concepts for each chapter. In a short 4 weeks, I had almost the whole book concept worked out. From there it was a matter of putting everything together. At the time of writing this chapter, it is currently printed out and taped on my living room wall so I can continue to arrange and work it out. Along the process of realizing your visions and goals, there's other plan pieces that will need to be figured out and added under the goal.

This brings me to a problem we have from watching too many movies. The music usually tells us when some defining moment is going on. The cinematography makes it obvious and usually something important is about to happen, whether it's negative or positive. The truth is real defining moments are in the small moments we experience each day. Every day is any given Sunday. Make a change by picking up a book to read instead of watching tv. Write down those thoughts you had for your own book. Spend 15 to 20 minutes exercising in the morning instead of hitting snooze. Get rid of that toxic negative friend in your life. Skip the bars to work on some of these goals you've written down. Help a stranger, take a class, learn a new skill, try and fail at new things, discover a talent. Those are the true defining moments!

Have you ever felt like you didn't have control of your life? I know I've spent the vast majority of my life just making the best of whatever situation I was living through. If this describes you, then find a vision and some goals. Put them down on paper and look at them regularly. Make sure your actions align toward that goal each day. Take some control and don't just wade around in the waters of life aimlessly.

For once in my life I have more direction and purpose than ever before. It's liberating! Do yourself (and the world by giving it the gifts of your best self) a favor and remove excuses from your mindset. Easier said than done, I know. There are times I react with an excuse to others and myself. I do my best to make sure I follow up with an objective look at the situation. Our reality is usually a reflection of our expectations. In case you sped past that in earlier chapters, I want to reiterate it. Our REALITY is usually a REFLECTION of our EXPECTATIONS. If your expectations are failure or not knowing where you are going, that is what you're going to get!

Getting comfortable in the uncomfortable is much easier said than done. Not letting fear rule my life has been a tremendous change. It really started at a chance at love two and a half years ago. I uprooted my entire life I had built over 25 years, and at age 30, left Georgia for New Jersey. I only knew my partner (now ex) when I moved up. I thought I would easily find a job after being a 30-year-old at the same company for 10 years, but it wasn't easy. I actually ended up in a totally different career field that has led to where I am now.

With my current work, I have a weird feeling that comes creeping in a lot. While out prospecting for new business, I get this physical sensation in my brain. It doesn't hurt but it also definitely doesn't feel good. I think it's related to anxiety or could even be the physical feeling of fear. It does slow me down. It does affect my ability to be fully efficient. However, it's eventually going to be less often and less intense. When I move even more out of my comfort zone into some of my larger goals, that feeling won't be as intense and easier to push through. Live a higher percentage of your life uncomfortably now, so you can live a higher percentage of it later in comfort. Some of that comfort is simply from the reaping of what is sewn. Some of that is from working, going through strife and discomfort, which has prepared you for tough situations.

Instead of being taken aback, reacting in an uncontrolled manner, and taking longer to get back on track (if you do at all) you will now be able to take the situation in stride. That's worth more than any comforts you could find in the lack of strife.

○○● Defining

I intended for this section to be simple closing thoughts, pieces I missed, or a highlights reel. I originally thought to entirely segregate the different parts and pieces. I ran into a complication. It was impossible to extract the pieces of the formula and stick entirely to that one idea or concept. The truth is it takes the whole formula for growth to grow. If you leave a piece off, it all crumbles. That means, unfortunately, it takes only a piece or two of the stagnation formula to infiltrate the growth and poison your growth.

Stagnation isn't a true mode for us. Stagnation is the same as moving backwards. Time and energy spent in stagnation is time and energy wasted as it could've been used to move forward. (don't confuse needed rest and stagnation) Let's pretend you're driving your car and three tires are rotating forward and one of them spinning backward. It's not going to turn out so well. It may be possible to keep the car straight and going forward but eventually that tire is going to pop. Then you're stuck on the side of the road with problems.

Look at the truly successful folks. I'm not talking about someone who makes a lot of money. I mean someone thriving in all areas. Personal life, business or career, finances, community impact, etc.

Analyze these awesome people and you will see some very common threads to pull on. They read and educate themselves frequently, take massive action, and practice being a visionary. They surround themselves with other successful people (feeds the energy and attitude). They don't let things like "It's never been done before," stop them (conquering the how). They are well aware of their "why."

The "successful" folks that "fall from grace" are the ones later we find out had started chasing the wrong why. Tiger Woods was, well, Tiger Woods. Then he began chasing the wrong why and, as of this writing, as far as we know life hasn't gone back to as good as it appeared to be at one time for him.

Running into this "problem" here at the wrap up section reassures me that I have put together a solid concept. I would think it is a comforting reassurance to you that this book is bringing information you can use and apply to your life to get where you want to be!

I am currently working on doing better at capturing my "why." I have made some progress on my willpower and stickability to push through tasks and must's. During my week, I come across moments that remind me exactly why I am pushing so hard at my goals. I still have yet to figure out how to get my "WHY" properly on paper or on a vision wall. My "how" wall is more populated right now.

Some people would have their "why" wall filled top to bottom and left to right with words and pictures that drive them to keep going. Others, like me, focus on the functional "how" of things. I put the definitions in each section for a purpose. I find when I am working through or on something, it is quite common that the solution lies in properly defining the situation and the problem. Oftentimes we are looking at the parts and pieces with a thought or mindset that is not clear or synonymous with how others see it. If the base of the problem isn't clear or the points of views don't line up, you lose synergy and proper direction. Let us get on the same page.

GOAL – The end toward which effort is directed.

FOCUS – Directed attention.

As an example of GOALS/FOCUS, in a soccer game, goals are what decide a win or lose. Not how much the team wanted to win. Not how much practice the team put in. Hell, not even how well the team played. You can have a team play technically better, but still lose. The goals that are scored are the difference. Life is certainly much less clear and simple. You don't lose at life when you miss your goals or fall a little short. In fact, as long as you learn from everything, good and bad, it's never really a miss.

In my life I have often been told, guided, led to, pressed upon, etc. to make goals. I disregarded it and just did the best I could in life. I have done decently well for myself from where I've started and what I was put through. I'm proud of all I have accomplished. Just doing decently well isn't quite enough, though. I now know and understand the importance of goals and how life changing they can be if you utilize them properly, meaning you don't use them as self-defeating tools. Don't beat yourself up for missing goals, and don't forget to formulate the goal clearly and with a timestamp.

I'm not the end all be all of goal setting and making. There isn't one perfect way to do it. As an example, the goal of this book was simple. Publishing was the headline, but first I had to create my outline. Below that was to write the book with an established end date. Below that was researching publishing. One main key to enjoy life is to just show up and try things. You'll be quite surprised where it will go and what you will do and try if you just start pushing yourself into a direction you have never gone before!

When you are setting and reverse engineering your goals into weekly and daily activities, you are either making goals to move you towards or away from something. Make sure you know which goal you are setting, a "toward" or "away from" goal. The definition of a goal says that it is the end for which an effort is directed. It's important to always make more goals or evolve your goals. You don't just arrive and you're done. Remember, you're always moving forward or backward. If nothing I have said above makes any difference, maybe this will. People who don't make goals usually work for those that do.

To end this section on a silly word turn, we'll define the word provision.

PROVISION - the act of providing.

That one is a little given. It's the B team and C team definitions here that really illustrates this word and my point.

B DEFINITION - The fact or state of being prepared beforehand.
C DEFINITION - A measure taken beforehand to deal with a need or contingency.

For B and C, you are using vision. You look at where you are and see what you need to get where you are going. In order to provide and give pro-vision to yourself, you better get some vision!

TIME - The measured or measurable period during which an action, process, or condition exists or continues.

Let's say you got a wild idea and decided to grow a Chinese bamboo tree. You plant the seeds and begin to nurture it to life. Did you know that the first year you wouldn't see any fruits of your labor? The week in and week out feeding, weeding, and watering of the soil, for...drum roll...nothing to show. In fact, year two, you still don't get results. But wait, there's more! Years three and four produce nada as well. What happens in year five is nothing short of amazing! In six short weeks, you get 80 feet of growth!

Did that plant grow 80 feet in six weeks or five years? Without the prior efforts before the plant grew above ground, there wouldn't be a plant. In reality, the plant grew 80 feet in 5 years, you just couldn't see it.

If you are spending your time, like I did for many years, just making the best of life then you will have some wins. You could quite possibly do just fine. If you're able to just meander into doing just fine, think of the possibilities of working with some control! Using my growth formula, even when you can't see or feel results, will help you in those years you don't see growth. At some point you will be able to look back and see it, but while you're blind, focus on the small pieces to build the whole of your life.

You can't save time. It ticks by second by second no matter what you do. You can only invest it, more or less, efficiently. When it comes to our equation, it's either being invested on the side for growth or for stagnation. None of us can live a perfect day every day. I implore you to do your best to keep the parts and pieces of the growth formula in place and spend time there. Do your best each day to not let stagnation pieces replace your growth. For example, living in the negative energy instead of positive energy. We all have 24 hours a day. Make them count as much as possible. One of the ways you can take control is with your attitude. Some of what makes an attitude is what you put out, but some of it is what you put in.

Make the best of your 24 hours with a little multitasking. You'll see in one of my appendixes a list of folks to listen to online or some other medium. While you're getting ready through your morning, on your commute, and even while sleeping have something playing. In less than a month I noticed a huge difference in my mood and mindset through the day. I got tremendously better with the whole "act vs react" through this method.

To practice time efficiency, I put my clothes together for the day and prep my food for throughout the day while I am waiting on my pre-workout to kick in. Then I have my breakfast cooking while exercising in the living room. I brush my teeth while making sure my dog has water. It sounds silly, but there is only 24 hours in a day!

ACTION - The accomplishment of a thing usually over a period of time, in stages, or with the possibility of repetition.
 B. An act of will

Some action is better than no action. However, massive action is what will give you the motion and inertia to get and keep going. Newton's first law of motion, sometimes referred to as the law of inertia, says an object at rest stays at rest and an object in motion stays in motion with the same speed and in the same direction unless acted upon by an unbalanced force. In other words, you can't drive a parked car.

You obviously want to work smarter, not harder. You want to be more efficient, not less efficient, towards your goals. That's why I included the idea of working on properly setting your goals and reverse engineering. You should look at them often and reassess. Why? You don't want all of that action to go to waste. If you have a man chopping wood and never stops to sharpen his ax, he is going to have problems. He may get stronger and faster as he goes along, but his production is going to lessen either way. Massive action is important. Make sure you do take time to sharpen your ax. Reading books, seeking counsel, resting, and a variety of other methods will help you mentally reset. We all need rest, try to more often than not make it "earned."

Your *actions* will dictate your *outcome*. Look in your calendar, journal, or search your short-term memory. What actions are there? That dictates your outcome. To take that a step further, your *actions* show your *belief* in your goals to be achieved.

Now pretend I am Quinten Tarantino and let's jump back. What determines your actions? Your *decisions* will dictate your *actions*. Instead of making decisions mindlessly, guard your mind and what influences your decisions. Take your mind back from social media and any other distractions. Make yourself present in your life and your *decisions*. Remember that your belief is actually just deciding to believe it. If decisions make the actions, then actions determine the outcome, which shows what you believe.

HOW - In what manner or way or what reason with what meaning at what price.

Part of the "HOW" is the vision. That's why I put focus first. Get your end goal clear and walk back some of the steps along the way that will make it happen. It is possible to reverse engineer your life. You won't have all of the pieces there. Some of it will be blank spaces that you will fill as you go along. Go as far as you can see, then when you get there, you can see more.

Some self-awareness is going to come into play here. Look at your goals you have written down and reverse engineered. What daily and weekly actions will it take to bring that into existence? Your daily rituals make your day and your future. If you're like me and know you are not someone that stays mentally organized easily, put together external tools to help you. For example, I have a thought wall in my living room. This chapter is currently on the wall in bits and pieces because I can't keep it in my head. When I am home, I have a habit of my brain losing the things I thought I needed to do. I have reminders all around, write things down throughout the day, or text myself so that when I get home, I can accomplish these tasks.

ENERGY - Dynamic quality, the capacity of acting or being active, a usually positive spiritual force, vigorous exertion of power, usable power

The thing about attitude and energy is it can really make or break a situation. The problem with our attitude is that it's usually based only on what we can see. If you've driven in New Jersey, you know what I mean when I say it's a state of blind spots. The street parking in many areas makes it near impossible to see if you have a clear shot of merging or crossing the road you're at. Just because it seems clear at first glance, doesn't mean that there isn't something just a little further out that won't be dangerous if you throttle it to cross the street.

Attitude can be very similar to a blind spot. For all we can see, the deal we are working on or the day we are in is all bad and we feel sucked dry from it. Keeping a good attitude through adversity can make all of the difference in the world. Your boss might notice that although the day is stressed beyond what anyone should have to deal with, you are taking it in stride with a smile. This sets the tone for those around you to follow. Be the thermostat of the room not the thermometer. That simple act can get you a promotion, partner status, into rooms and conversations that you otherwise would have missed!

Let's take a different approach from the NJ traffic visual, since getting T-boned in traffic isn't exactly a positive note to leave off on. There's been plenty of situations I've been nervous over and feared and went in with a nervous attitude. The person across from you can feel that and it makes them uncomfortable. I've also spent plenty of time stressed or nervous before a situation only for it to be perfectly fine in the end.

One tactic I have been using and trying to keep at the forefront of my mind is viewing the physical manifestations of nervousness as excitement.

At its core, the two are similar. Ask Michael Phelps how he felt before a qualifying swim and he would probably say something like sweaty palms, butterflies in the stomach, and brain moving faster than he can keep up with. Ask someone that has to give a group presentation how they feel, and will probably list the same physical symptoms. The difference being Phelps is going to call it excitement and the other person will call it nervousness. So, the next time you are trying to tackle something and feel worried about it, keep telling yourself you are just excited. Think about the parts of the situation you are actually excited for. The outcome, the relief of getting past it, or whatever it is to get your brain to wrap around the excited aspect of the situation.

I recently had a presentation I was nervous about and used this exact trick to get through it. Sure, I still had a bit of nervousness, but it was very quickly that I got comfortable with my presentation. I had someone in the audience take notes on what I did right and what I could keep in mind to do differently. Surprisingly, he said that I appeared very confident. Now in the first 2 minutes or so of the presentation, I felt like I wasn't at the top of my game, but to everyone I seemed cool as a cucumber the entire time. I have no doubt that getting myself in the mindset that I am excited and ready for this made a huge difference in my ability to perform at top quality!

As a closing thought on attitude, you deserve the best of you. Everyone you meet deserves the best of you as well. Whether that is the person at the start, middle, or end of your day. If you are not a "morning person", you might just be in the wrong time zone. Maybe you just need to be in Hawaii, you know, for the time zone.

Okay, but seriously, if you are not a "morning person" but right as rain in the evening, it is your responsibility to figure out how to give the world the "evening person" you are in the early hours. When I go out prospecting for new business, it doesn't matter how many rejections I get, it is my responsibility to give the last person I talk to the best attitude and energy I have. You're only cheating yourself out of opportunity by succumbing to the idea that you just can't be on point at a certain time in the day.

PURPOSE - The reason for which something is done or created or for which something exists. Also, A person's sense of resolve or determination.

For a large portion of my adult life I have heard people say that if you can figure out the *why*, you will be able to figure out the *how*. They're not wrong, but I don't think it is the prerequisite. Although I generally have a purpose behind what I say or do, I'm not always able to define it. There are a ton of *how's* I have figured out and completed without being able to clearly define the *why*. The best reason I can give is there was something innate that drove me through. There are those who say that if you have a strong enough purpose, you can "fake it till you make it."

They're not exactly wrong, but this formula is like beauty. It is in the eye of the beholder. I have, in my days, accomplished things with innate drive or without a real sense of purpose. I have other undertakings I couldn't accomplish because I was borrowing someone else's purpose. That said, I will implore you to search and find your true purpose for the current season. Try not to get too married to it, as in life seasons change.. When you find something or someone that truly drives you, it amplifies all other parts of the taking control side of the formula!

If you haven't found it yet, do not fret! Colonel Sanders wasn't Mr. KFC until after 65. I don't wish for it to take that long for any of us, but it could. Other than soul searching, deep conversation, or schooling, the real only way to find purpose is to just experience life and things. Develop a zest and zeal to get off your tail end and go live. Eventually you will find something that stirs your soul and emotions. It will give you the feeling that today was definitely worth getting out of bed.

Even as confused and uncontrollable and alien as feelings have been to me in the past, when I come across situations that are a piece of my *why*, I feel something. Once you have figured out what it is, do your best to experience and see it as much as possible. If material items are not your thing, posting cars and houses up on your mirror will be a waste. If your purpose comes from being able to buy your mom a house, then that is something you can use to create motivation. Take her out to lunch and ask about what she would like in a house. Draft a dream home with her and I'm willing to be that will help. You need more than just one little material thing to represent your *why*.

You always need to evolve and develop as well. A person with something to live for is more likely to keep doing so! If you aren't aware of the story of Dick and Rick Hoyt, I recommend watching their videos. Their story centers around a father who couldn't run an Iron Man but was suddenly able to when his physically incapacitated son told him he felt like he was running after they did a 5k together. He has now done hundreds of Iron Man events with his son in tow to help him feel alive. His *why* is stronger than most of us can come up with, but also has pushed him to superhuman limits.

Before I leave the "taking control" side and dive into the "losing control" side of the equation, there is a very important note that I want to cover. This equation is 24/7. You know what 24/7 covers? Weekends! You can't just play the first half of the game; you have to show up on the field for the second half and give it all you have! Gerrain Jones used this metaphor— brush your teeth three times a day every day for five years. Then stop for a week. How is that going to go for you? The parts and pieces of the formula are always at play!

This past weekend was an extended weekend. Well, for some. I worked 6 days of the week, wrote on Sunday and for the holiday on the Monday I wrote as well. I treated Monday like a weekend day. I didn't listen to any mindset material Saturday, Sunday, or Monday. I didn't play my usual sleep meditation training either. (in this season as of this writing I need those two frequently to keep my headspace right) Monday afternoon, I napped, and Monday night, I didn't sleep well. My mind was running a million miles a minute thinking about some of my various projects. Classic anxiety.

I went out into my day Tuesday with a "not very on top of the world" feeling. Very dour compared to the previous week's emotional levels. Thankfully, due to lots of practice and implementing good habits, I was able to push it aside and stride through it. To help, I listened to some mindset videos I should have through the weekend to help me get in the right mindset throughout the day. The more you ingrain the habits of taking control of your mind and life, the more FULLY in the "taking control" side of the equation you will live.

The word that comes to mind is RELENTLESS. You must be dedicated and relentless about living a life where you control what is in your control. Since you can only control what you think, say, and do, it is important to control these things at every moment. With that said, from time to time even the best of us are going to act in a way that is out of control. Everyone experiences fear, the lack of desire to do something that is required, or a "woke up on the wrong side of the bed" day. If you practice the discipline of relentlessly thinking, acting, and saying things that are in control, the harder times and days will happen less and less, and bouncing back from them will be far easier. We must remember to apologize to those around us when we do lose control or have that sharp tone. Last Sunday I was running around doing a few things I had to do at church and twice when I spoke to someone I afterwards had to catch my tone may have been off. I had to then go apologize and clarify.

PROCRASTINATION - to put off intentionally the doing of something that should be done

There is a great book to read about this topic (it's short, so don't put it off.) It's by Brian Tracy and called *Eat the Frog*. Consider the following hypothetical situation (Okay, you got me, based on real life. Only once though. Maybe twice.) The alarm goes off at 5 AM. There is an important presentation to give. Since I stayed up late with fruitless activity, I am drowsy. Also, I had to move my wake-up time and lost out on my exercise time, which helps provide fresh oxygen to the body, give the mind and soul a confidence boost, and just increases overall health. I forgot to meal prep. Now I'm not able to stick to my healthier eating plan, nor did I have time to get the exercise in.

"I knew I would do that," I tell myself. I'm not only letting myself fall off the wagon, I'm running myself over with the wagon. There's most likely going to be traffic I don't normally get due to unforeseen road work. There will probably be ice on the windshield and because I procrastinated on getting gas earlier, I guess I will have to do it now or chance being stranded. Since I'm now frantic and on edge about making it on time, I can't be calm and prepared.

I could keep going on with this snowball of a nightmare for the start of a day, but you get the point. All I had to do was spend a little bit of time in prep work to save time of high anxiety. I will probably at some point beat myself for it as well. Just more salt on the wound of the boss beating you up for it. I don't care if it is using Mel Robbins' 5 second countdown and act method or sheer will power, find something that works. If you're constantly playing catch up from letting the dishes pile up, you can never get ahead. Also, something will inevitably start to smell bad and no one likes that!

Those are realistically surface deep examples of the effects of procrastination. I am not one for living on the surface and it is certainly not why I wrote this book. My mom can be a lesson to each of you indulging in these words of wisdom and experience. She had a brother that passed away sometime around when they were in high school. She is still sometimes effected by his loss. He died in a house fire one night. She was pregnant with me at the time, so I've escaped death at least once in my life, but her brother Bob didn't. Unfortunately, his body was found not far from his window. It was the smoke that got him.

Earlier that day he needed a part for his bike to repair it. She procrastinated and said she'd take him another day. Since he died that night she lives with the regret and guilt of letting him down. I've seen her break down into tears when fire trucks rush by. At the time we procrastinate, it is usually not going to feel like it is a big deal. The problem is we don't really know when it will be. Do your best in every moment so that you can always look back and know that you tried!

Train yourself to be present in your decisions (*self-awareness déjà vu*). Don't just meander through life without considering the effects of your consequences. My mom would have never guessed her situation was going to happen. When you go to procrastinate, firstly you have to realize it is what you're doing. We can do it so easily and not realize we are procrastinating. The good next step is an honest pro and con session. The KEY here is to ask your rational brain, not your emotional brain. Is it even a task that should be on my list? Is now really the time or is there a good reason for it to be done later? Will this negatively affect someone else? Will this negatively affect me? How so? Is it simple and easy, and if so, why wouldn't I just get it done to get it out of the way?

What I'm saying is to not just let yourself be on misguided autopilot. Challenge yourself. Challenge your thoughts and decisions. It's these little daily decisions that make the difference in your life so don't give yourself a hall pass on them!

I will throw in a word of caution; *extremes are not good.* If a tennis player uses the same racket too long, the strings will wear out and their strikes will lose efficacy. Your mind and body are the same as that racket. While procrastinating isn't good, you can swing the other way and go too much. Even the busiest high producers in the world need a moment to recharge.

APATHY - absence or suppression of passion, emotion, or excitement; lack of interest in or concern for things that others find moving or exciting.

Before looking this word up in the dictionary, I thought it meant to be lazy. I wrote in the introduction you will find definitions in this book for this very reason. It was when speaking with one of my "wise counsel members" that I discovered apathy isn't someone being lazy. It's more a lack of drive.

I've had thousands of conversations, one of the topics being what someone did and why. The overwhelming majority was doing what they fell into. If that is what they are gifted for, great. All is well. It's when someone isn't doing what they are gifted in or created for that they can slip down the slope of becoming a shell of a human. No drive. No purpose. Going through the motions.

I don't want the wrong idea to be portrayed here. I am not saying that everyone should be writing a book or trying to change the world, or that anyone is better than anyone else. It doesn't necessarily have to be grandiose. Your purpose can be a run-of-the-mill everyday living. Working an honest day's work, providing for a family, and being a conducive member to society in the "normal" ways. What I am talking about is the person who has it in their heart to accomplish a particular purpose, yet they don't.

It could be that run-of-the-mill everyday purpose. Pursuing a career as a counselor, a plumber, insurance, public works, etc. One of the many folks I spoke with was a teacher for six years. It got in her heart to become a financial advisor. She made the change and as of this writing, is still in the difficult beginning phases. She is incredibly happy and fulfilled in it, as stressful as it can be.

I personally believe that logic and emotions are complete opposites. If we use the metaphor of a boat, there is the steering wheel and the engine. If someone is living all in emotion, that is like a boat with the engine full throttle and no steering wheel. It's getting places but without control. Most likely it's going to run aground, and if it is a cheesy movie, there will be a huge explosion. If you are living in all logic and no emotion, that is like having a steering wheel and no engine. You know how to control it if there is something to control. It takes a blend of the two. Logic and emotion.

We can live in logic too much and ignore the things we have in us because it doesn't make logical sense. On the flip side, we can get so caught up chasing something emotional that we haven't taken time to take any inventory and try to calculate the best path.

I say all of this to remind you to blend together logic and emotion, and make sure you are living in-purpose. You may not discover right away what that purpose is, and this is okay. If you go too long with a purpose inside you, suppressing it, you can find yourself becoming one of those shells of a human. Stuck with an absence of passion, emotion, or excitement. You might have a lack of interest in or concern for things that others find moving or exciting. That definition sounds like what most would consider depression. Depending on the source, 12% to 16% of the population are on antidepressants. Let's spread the word to move the number of people on antidepressants due to apathy down!

NEGATIVE - lacking positive qualities, marked by features of hostility, withdrawal, or pessimism that hinder or oppose constructive treatment or development

Have you ever, or even now, had a toxic friend or coworker? You know who I am talking about. Negative Nancy or Ned. It doesn't matter what happens, it is always raining where they are. Ned or Nancy makes sure that it is raining at least 30 feet around them, too, because misery loves company. When they are finding ways to complain about the uncomplainable, (I recall a time this was me for a time and was thankfully called out on it to stop the spiral) remember that an empty can rattles the most.

If you are that person, know that this is how your friends and coworkers see you; the empty can rattlin'. When you walk around the corner, they can feel your negative ooze get on them and they are ready to run! If you're a positive person dealing with one of these negative people, I will not suggest forsaking them totally, but if you lay down with dogs you get fleas. Give them the positive energy and vibes but know your time and worth. If they are not changing, do your best to minimize your time around them until they are ready to change. Just set the example from a distance and sew your energy where it will grow.

DISTRACTIONS - an object that directs one's attention away from something else, the act of distracting or the state of being distracted; *especially* mental confusion.

We all have time for what we make time for. You can be too tired to clean the house and justify sitting around the house with Netflix. Five minutes later, your friend calls up about going to a restaurant and you

103

magically aren't tired anymore. That is an example of a distraction from doing what needs to be done. I am not condoning cutting all friends off and only focusing on tasks, just to be clear. There's always going to be more to do. I need time with friends. It recharges the batteries. I need some down time from work, self-improvement, thinking, writing, and even fun. We were not created to just work like drones. In all things, some balance is good.

I've tried to help guide someone to a healthier diet in the past. This person would say that they haven't really eaten that bad this week, so there was no harm in getting a cupcake. They had pizza 5 days before. Sugar filled candies after dinner each night. They thought Italian ices were healthy, but they are loaded with sugar. If this person had tracked what they were eating, they'd know they were way out of whack on their nutrition. However, they didn't, and they quickly forgot every bad thing they ate.

Forgetfulness is always going to justify what your emotion is telling you. *"Well, I can go to the movies since I worked so hard this week,"* you might tell yourself. If you analyzed your week, you'd be surprised. It was actually filled with tv, video games, social media, gossip, and general inefficient use of time. This is why goals are important. If you put your goals down and reverse engineer for the track you can keep focused on them. Then with intentional purpose and direction, you are not spending the bulk of your time in unfruitful endeavors.

EXCUSES - to try to remove blame from, to serve as an excuse for.

All parts of the stagnation side of the formula is detrimental to your life, but excuses really pull you out of reality and trap you in a cycle. You can mislead yourself to live in a faux world. If you are in a battle and not battling the true enemy, you can never win. Excuses have you battling a false enemy. Every time you enact the skin of a lie and stuff it with reason, you are fooling yourself. If you keep making an excuse as to why you can't do something, you are going to get great at making excuses. Think about that for a moment. When it is really something important that you're avoiding, you know you're making excuses. There's a little something there that makes you hesitate or skip a beat before moving along with the excuse.

It's not a big deal if it is simple tasks that don't make a major difference in life. The dishes stack up a little, the mail backs up a little, maybe there are more dust bunnies than should be around the house. The problem really kicks in when you get so good at excuses that you don't realize you are making them. Which then leads to making excuses in places that you really can't afford to. I can put off getting gas one more day and run out on the way home. I can tell myself I've been on this job long enough I can skip certain duties one day and I'm fired the next week. I can say I didn't eat that bad this week so pancakes for breakfast, fast food for lunch, and red velvet cake after dinner will be okay, then end up having a heart attack during sleep.

Don't allow yourself to be a victim of these lies. They will rob you of your future. Sacrifice who you are today for who you need to be tomorrow. If who you are today is an excuse person, let's swap out that excuse for some action!

I've found most often it comes down to two main excuses: resources or fear. Resources being time, money, support, etc. After spending some years networking, I have found there is more assistance than we might know out there. There are endless resources for financial backing, education, and business loans. Likewise, there's a lot of support for people held back by fear, through therapy, online communities, chambers of commerce, and more. If you're looking for it hard and true to heart enough, you will find the support.

ooo Reflection

Here is where you can put steps towards the pioneering mindset. Danny Boone, let's ask some questions of ourselves. What have you read in this chapter that is a fresh new concept or idea? Write it down and put it on your thought wall. Were there some things that you see as a personal strength or didn't know about before? What pieces of the stagnation formula are getting transposed into your growth formula? What can you do to pour fuel on those fires? How about your weaknesses? Were there some that came to mind you already knew of or now see that could use some work? What metaphorical sticks can you gather to start building a fire with those weaknesses?

Here's a hint. We were not created to be alone. Isolation is a killer. (I wrote this chapter well before the 2020 Covid-19 outbreak. Now those two sentences have a whole new meaning.) I love people and being around people. I do, however, tend to isolate myself when it comes to needing help or guidance. There're many times in my life, if I had gotten proper counsel or assistance, I would have had much less strife. It is hard to cultivate in yourself something you don't have or didn't have a good example of to emulate. However, someone else can lend their talent and in turn help plant and grow what you didn't have!

Being aware of your weaknesses alone won't fix them and you shouldn't try to work on them alone. Seek people who have qualities you want to develop so some osmosis can happen. If the how is your strength, build your centers of influence with some folks that have a great positive attitude, and great at visualizing and painting a why picture. Don't fight them, but instead learn to integrate their strengths and emulate them.

Chapter 4

Belief

> *"Some people like to say if I see it, I can believe it. NO, NO, NO. If you believe it, you can see it!"* - Les Brown

Belief - a state or habit of mind in which trust or confidence is placed in some person or thing, something that is accepted, considered to be true, or held as an opinion : something believed, conviction of the truth of some statement or the reality of some being or phenomenon especially when based on examination of evidence

Faith - allegiance to duty or a person, sincerity of intentions, firm belief in something for which there is no proof, something that is believed especially with strong conviction

Perspective - a mental view or prospect, the interrelation in which a subject or its parts are mentally viewed, the capacity to view things in their true relations or relative importance

Our reality is a mirror of our true expectations. Our expectations are what we truly believe. Don't believe me? I'll prove it.

Many of us say that we don't care what others think, then we check the mirror 15 times a day to make sure our image is perfect. We post only the best pictures of ourselves online. We stress about how we phrase our opinions to everyone we talk to, stranger or not, because of how it could make us look. Those actions don't line up with the words, "I don't care what others think." In reality, most of the people who claim they don't care don't follow through with their actions.

If you want to know what you really believe, start analyzing your actions. What you do reveals the true internal thoughts that you never dare speak and will confirm what you actually care about. In my high school years, I took a zero on a project just to avoid speaking in front of my peers. In my twenties I imagined myself being a public speaker, but never sought out opportunities to do so. These days, speaking in front of a crowd is a regular occurrence for me. This shift happened because I experienced an evolution of belief, and in turn, I made the right efforts to make my belief a reality. It wasn't an overnight change, but it happened!

In that vein, what you believe is what you express. If you notice that the choices you make, the thoughts you have, or the words you speak aren't conducive to what you want, you need to change how and what you are expressing. Like I said, what you express reinforces what you believe. Glance back to Chapter One: Pitfalls where I mention that how you behave affects you. When you feel angry or depressed, try to smile or laugh, and not just for a brief minute. Keep it up through-out the day, even if you don't see or feel a reason to smile. See how mindfully choosing positive reactions changes how you feel at that moment.

There's a common character dynamic we often see in movies and sometimes even see in real life of the Upper and Downer. Character A, who is always negative and stressed, is downtrodden and they go to

Character B, who points out the positives and makes them feel better. Usually, their improved mood can be attributed to two things; they took their mind off of stress for a few minutes and when they returned to the problem, they reshaped the perspective.

Now let's expand that to a larger level of thought. Do you feel like you can't accomplish something? Do you think it is too much for you or that you can't "be enough" for it? Those who truly believe they can't succeed won't try, while those who have an inkling of hope that they can succeed will try, even if it's only half-heartedly. Unfortunately, just trying at minimal effort isn't always enough to make it work. Still, they may possibly get lucky and find success regardless. Even a broken clock is right twice a day! On the bright side, some activity and effort is always better than no activity, even if it doesn't always yield results. The problem is if a person with already little hope doesn't look at the situation the right way, it will reinforce that "I knew I couldn't" mentality inside them.

What does it look like for someone who believes they are going to "make it work", that they will succeed no matter what? They are the ones who are going all in. They are going to research, struggle and struggle more, act and move, find resources (not reasons to quit), and keep moving toward their goal. If they realize that their goal isn't what is best for them or maybe realistically isn't achievable, then they still move on to the next thing with a strong sense of ferocity, intention, and belief. Sometimes giving up is the best course of action. Those who fully believe in themselves know that this doesn't mean failure, but rather, a new door for them to open elsewhere with newly gained experiences and wisdom.

Then there are those folks that sit on the side lines, looking at the players, thinking, "how are they doing this," "how did they know they could get here", "must be nice to be that confident and without doubt". Here is the secret to the success of those confident and seemingly invincible players: they did doubt. They were not 100% for 100% of the time. They were likely 100% sure at least 51% of the time.

This is great news! Perfection is impossible to achieve, but we just covered that we don't have to have perfect faith and belief to get what and where we want! Notice in the definition of faith it says sincerity of intentions, not confidence of intentions.

There are a couple of themes that go through this entire book. One of them is action. Belief is an action. Depression, while also a state, is an action. Faith, likewise, is an action. For example, we have faith that gravity is going to continue existing tomorrow and the next day and for as long as we're alive. If we didn't, everyone would be walking around with a weight belt with little cannon balls tied to it so that we didn't float away whenever gravity stopped existing. Silly idea, but it's true! Many of us look silly when we have faith in something that is false.

If you are reluctant to try something, decipher if it is simply fear of trying something new or if you truly don't believe you are going to succeed. It's important to know the difference. If what you're doing is, say, speaking in front of a group or some other arduous upcoming task and you determine that you are simply nervous, well, there's ways around that! You can try relaxing breathing techniques or psych yourself up, practice until it is as common as breathing, encouraging yourself to be excited instead of nervous. Find your confidence in what you know rather than focusing on what you don't know. Think of previous times that you did something new but was able to figure it out. You can visualize things going the way you want. These are actions you can take to overcome your nerves instead of focusing on fear. I'm not saying you'll magically be in perfect condition mentally and not still feel some of the physical constraints, but you will be better prepared and nimble to accomplish the task.

However, if your core belief is that you can't do it and you have no faith in yourself, that is a drastic problem. This lack of faith is going to manifest into all sorts of additional problems that you are more likely to listen to, and ultimately, allow to dictate what you do.

What I am trying to say is that having faith in the ability to succeed looks a certain way. Likewise, faith that you are going to fail looks a certain way. Study those that have not succeeded in their endeavors and see what that looks like. Do the same for those you consider successful. Emulate their body posture, speaking tones and rhythms, how they move, facial expressions, etc. That isn't to say that you have to become another person, but rather, take these successful mannerisms and make them your own.

It is possible to be unsure about something but outwardly show confidence regardless, ultimately creating a successful outcome. On a few occasions when I've had to speak in front of crowds, I didn't always feel sure about how well it was going. I didn't feel successful, but I kept talking and moving as though I did, as though everything was going exactly as I had planned it. Afterward, the feedback I've received from people has been that I look very comfortable speaking and do a great job. For years, I've envisioned myself speaking in front of others and feel it is what I am destined to do. My drive to do well helps me to push past any temporary nervous feelings, and the preparation habits I've created helps to ensure success. This is all part of moving in belief.

I would not be doing my job right if I didn't acknowledge the elephant in the room. More often than not, life will not look like the success you want. Most of your time will be spent on the journey toward success, the transformation of where you are to where you envision yourself, rather than at the destination. This means that you are not going to see what you want most of the time. This means living by faith, not by sight. Also, you have to be willing to edit your perception and expectation of what that journey and destination looks like. If you get too married to your own expectations, the journey and destination can become unfulfilling and steal your energy and the wind from your sails to keep going to the next thing.

What have you accepted as your beliefs and faith? What have you accepted as outcomes, as how your journey will look, as your identity, as what you perceive reality to be versus what it is? Has this book helped you to see outside of your forest? What disciplines are you going to change in thoughts, words and actions? Will Smith said he believes self-discipline is self-love. He believes it to be true, and as we can see in his life, successes, passion, and zest for life, he follows through with it. Have you believed discipline is a bad word? Have you only believed that you would live in scarcity and failure? By the way, living in abundance doesn't only mean we have a lot of money or fame. How do you define abundance? How do you define success?

These are your questions to answer, honestly and without any judgment toward yourself, as you take your next step on your journey.

Appendix A

The Question Train, All Aboard!!!!

First step is managing expectations. Keep in mind that if you're not used to analyzing your true motives below the surface of decisions, you're not going to be a natural at it overnight. Give yourself some grace to build the habit. Secondly, not every single decision needs to be looked at or immediately needs thought about. No one has a perfect walkthrough guide of their life and we're all learning as we go. Lastly, it's impossible for me to make this an exhaustive list of questions that could pertain to everything you will encounter. These are starting points to curtail to your life.

If you've never seen the video of Simon Sinek, *Start with Why*, go watch it. Then get in the habit of questioning why. Create a journal to track your thoughts and answers to these questions!

WHY

- Why am I doing/thinking this?
- Am I doing this to serve some desire grounded in seeking pleasure/avoiding pain/filling a void, is it rooted in serving a purpose, or the habits and customs I've created that are no longer relevant to who I have become and seeking to become?
- Will this serve me/my purpose/my journey of seeking purpose/others in a way that is constructive or destructive?

TIMING

- Is this the time to work on this or is there a higher priority to focus on now?
- If I let this go unchecked is it going to spin out of control?
- If not now, when is the time? Make clear circumstances to describe when to work on it. This is covered in the Pitfalls chapter, "The Carrot and The Stick." Don't get caught in that pitfall, instead declare indicators as to what step in the process it is and work to it. Metaphorically speaking, I'm at half a tank of fuel in the car now, when I get to the quarter tank marker, I'm stopping to refuel. As a real life example, I wanted to move back to home from where I was living. I put parameters of what milestones/priorities were completed in my life to be time for the move. Here is why it is important to not get too married to how something has to go. That actually ended up getting changed due covid and my employer selling my division. In this case it was all better than I could have hoped for on how everything played out.

WHAT/HOW

- **What is this?**
  A habit I have that needs to be replaced? (habits are rarely quit, they're generally replaced by design or happenstance if design is lacking.)
- **What will I replace it with?**
  How am I going to ensure that I follow through? I.E. what mechanisms will I put in place to help me? Micro real life example, if I forget to take medication in the morning I set an alarm or reminder in my phone to help me remember until it's natural.

- **A response to a situation?**
  Is this a common situation I find myself in? If so, how will I stop letting myself fall into this situation?

- **What happened? How can I look at it differently?**

The previous questions pertain more to moving forward, but we also need to look at the past. Here is a brief story; for at least 5 years after finding my dad, I lived with this idea that I would have been a better person (mostly more confident and successful) if he had always been around. Then, in a counseling session after a friend passed away, this came up to the counselor. She challenged my belief. She said I didn't know that and if I was going to live in "what if land," I had to equally apply the level of positive and negative potential outcome. I vehemently disagreed and left without a changed mind, until it marinated for about three days later and I realized she was right.

I could perceive all the physical and mental abuse I went through in my earliest years as experiences that were stolen from me, or I could look at it as experiences that were given to me. Ultimately, I chose the latter. While bad at the time, my experiences gifted me the ability to reach the unreachable, change the unchangeable, and understand those who feel misunderstood.

What perspectives have you held onto your entire life that need to change? What events do you look at as defining moments and define them in the worst possible way? What in your heart is poison that you have allowed to sit there by telling yourself false narratives about it instead of allowing it to be medicine that you can give to others? Finding purpose in your pain is one of the best gifts you can give to the world and those right around you.

WARNING: this should lead to giving forgiveness to people where you need to. Giving freedom to you and those you forgive. Which can then lead to you apologizing where you need to.

Important thing I have learned about forgiveness. Forgiveness does not mean there has to be reconciliation. It is for you to not have a weight and poison carried around (forgiveness is an action not a feeling. You may have to do the act and later it will fully sink in and let the weights go from inside). Forgiveness is not saying it was right or okay the trespass against you, but saying you nor the other person has to carry the weight of it anymore.

If this person doesn't change the actions that led to the hurt and is going to continue in the behavior, it may be necessary to cut off their access and ability to hurt you.

Appendix B

Habits

1. **Smile and move** happily and the action will produce the result! If you can't do it now, you won't be able to do it later. How many rich and famous have committed suicide and been in and out of rehab? It's not wealth and power that makes one happy. It's one's decision to be happy despite any facts or situation.
2. **The best way to accomplish Habit One is through gratitude.** To be great, you have to be grateful! Before you get out of bed say an item or two you are grateful for. Obviously, there will be repeats, but try to not repeat the same from the day before. For those who have a hard time with this, I will give some examples:
    - Life. You're not dead yet, so you have much more left to do to be a good impact.
    - Family/Friends. Those who have supported you as well as those that didn't. Each one serves as inspiration and lessons to learn from.
    - Wisdom that you have learned and will learn in the future.
    - Gifts you have discovered and will discover. We all have them, it's up to us to discover them and use them

- Basic needs met, such as a house and food. Even if it isn't what you desire or aspire to one day have/enjoy, you still have shelter and nourishment.
- Hardships, because it's in those you learn and gain the most.
- Learning how to let go, even when it's painful.
- Time spent with those you have lost. As an example, I found my dad at 18 and only got to meet his dad once before he passed. I am so grateful that I got the time I did with him that it overshadows any grief or bitter about not having as much time as I wished I did.

3. **Videos after waking up.** Your mind is most susceptible to programming when you first get up. It can also be a tone setter for the day. Twenty to thirty minutes of taking in the right words and messages will change your life. It will be so subtle you won't notice at first, but you'll look back and see where it's changed. (Appendix C has suggestions)

4. **Community/Networking.** I say this most with the business world in mind but can certainly apply to general social situations. Be early to pitch in and help, be one of the last to leave to help, and catch up with everyone you can. If you see someone by themselves, talk to that person. Open with, "What brings you here?" or "What has been your favorite part of this week/month/event?" to start the conversation. The treasure is in the follow up, make sure you call or email if the situation calls for it.

5. **Make decisions now that your future self will appreciate.** I asked my Godson to put his clothes away, which I had laid on

the bed so that they were easy to put up. He stacked them in a place they didn't go, which would have gotten in the way of him getting ready for school and likely would have made a mess in his rush to get ready. He would have been angry with his past self if I didn't catch it. Prepare as much as possible. Do the little things that work towards your goal today so that tomorrow you are not beating yourself up.

6. **Read affirmations in the mirror.** We are what we tell ourselves we are. Too easily do we say, "I'm dumb," or some other horrible affirmation during the day. Write different quotes on your bathroom mirror each week. Read them to yourself. Put in the good words your subconscious needs to hear!

7. **Goals!** Think about, focus on, adjust as necessary, and most importantly create and have them! There are books and programs to help you with SMART goals and crafting them. Get those resources and help you with goals.

Appendix C

You Get Out What You Put In: Videos to Bombard Yourself With.

As of the writing of this book, I am not affiliated with any companies or individuals whose quotes may be used. I'm not paid to mention them, they are simply what I used to start the shift in mindsets and keep them going. Most of my resources come from Youtube or other public online platforms. Below are individuals I highly recommend watching:

- **Tom Bileyu**
  The man has a great story. One of the founders of Quest Protein. He has a few different YouTube channels to checkout. He is the modern day Napoleon Hill. Always interviewing high producers in different realms to learn more and more of their mindset and how-to's. We get the luxury of seeing the interviews!

- **Ted Talks**
  You can find Ted Talks on any topic.

- **Motiversity on Youtube**
  Incredible brain and mindset fuel! Listen to a video or two first thing in the morning everyday!

- **Dr. Billy Alsbrooks**
  An incredible man with a level of transparency that is quite refreshing! He gives a message and at an intensity that will help you dial up yours.

- **Matthew McConaughey**

He has a speech he gave at a college commencement that is about forty minutes long. That is one amazing speech with so much wisdom pouring out of it. Listen and take notes.

- **Be Inspired**
- **MotivationHub**
- **Mulligan Brothers**
- **Success Archive**
- **Les Brown**
- **Tony Robbins**
- **Eric Thompson**
- **Eddie Pinero**

For my fellow Christian brothers and sisters, or anyone curious of my biblical references, Jesus and his love and salvation available to you, these pastors tackle the important items and do it well as far as I have seen as of this writing. They are transparent and great teachers.

- **Michael Todd - Transformation Church**
  Every single sermon. Truly transformed me. He is number one on this list for a reason.

- **Daniel Groves - Hope City**
  This guy is a cross between an amazing, wise, revelatory, transparent, humble preacher and a comedian. Easy to listen to and to apply his teachings.

- **Steven Furtick of Elevation Church**
  Every single sermon.

- **Jimmy Evans**
  If you need some heart healing - that man has the sermons for it.

- **Ben Stuart - Passion City Church**
  Just learning of him, but everything so far is stellar.

Acknowledgements

Thanks dad and mom for having fun the wrong way in college. I don't condone anyone else going the same route, however God has worked it out well for me in the long run. I appreciate the support.

Thanks Brandon for your faith in me and always seeing me as better than I am.

The Phillips family, y'all have been integral to my enjoyment of life, survival, and thriving. You made some amazing god kids that I get the joy of watching/being involved with maturing into adults, and I look forward to the countless more laughs and life milestones together. My birth certificate doesn't say Phillips, but y'all are blood to me.

The Entwisle's, you found and accepted me in a life transition. Together with Byrnes, Buttimer, and Brian I for the first time began to really break out of my shell. It was an extremely tough year that each of you in one way or another was integral to me not only enduring it, but having some safety and joy to escape to.

Manny Goncalves. You are the man! Literally, it's in your name. You get it. Work and play hard. Treat people with respect. Pay it forward. If I ever become a dad, I took many notes from your parenting.

I moved to NJ for a relationship I shouldn't have pursued. I found myself without my friends I grew up with and the relationship was a recipe for disaster for her and I. Thankfully through her I found your friendship. Our conversations made me a better person. I was always super broke and you footed my bill many times so I could be there. From you, I got a vision for a different life than what my past had dictated, with the encouragement to do it. I am excited to see the adventures you get to experience in the years to come! I look forward to the day when I have a summer home up there so we can enjoy the cigars and a port, dominos, the water, steaks on the grill, and awesome conversation frequently!

Jason Martin. My Jamaican brotha from anotha motha. We've both learned and helped each other so much! You've helped me stretch beyond who I was and really walk towards who God created me to be. Iron sharpens Iron. I'm really excited to see your continued growth, transformation, and impact everywhere you go.

Jessica Sullivan. You didn't know me from the next guy but was quick to be helpful and insightful. You're kind, strong, insightful, a visionary, and all-around awesome! I appreciate your efforts and friendship. I look forward to see all the new ideas you come up with and employ.

Rosemary Rosencrans. One of the strongest angels God has put in my path. I'm grateful for your kind words, insightful truth, and amazing presence. Keep being awesome!

Adam, Shawn, David, Brian, Travis. We haze each other but we are all there to support each other in our weird way. I know if I needed help any of you would do what you could. We don't get into the shenanigans that the teen versions of ourselves did, for the most part anyway.

Parag Nevatia, founder of EZ Funding Solutions. THE PERSON to talk to if you own a business and want or need assistance on bankability, franchising, credit, business plans, etc. I put an ad in my book for him here because he is amazing at what he does and for those that need his help should seek him out if by chance they see this. It's due to his awesome personality and a couple conversations we had that this book was written. He didn't even know at the time he was sparking the idea, but he did. He changed the course of my life with a few words and didn't even know it at the time. Thank you sir!

About the Author

Christopher Phillips Hennes is a student of the school of life. He combines his faith with his life experiences to guide others as they grow and flourish. He is passionate about healing, transformation, habits, the thermostat being at 70, and Graycee, his golden lab mix.

He has helped folks with self-awareness, relationships, forgiveness, and more. While he offers wisdom and guidance on a myriad of topics, one piece is key to his success. He has an innate ability of helping people in doing one very important thing. Helping them get to the root and heart of matters.

Made in United States
Orlando, FL
27 January 2024